LEICESTERSHIRE

CLIMBS

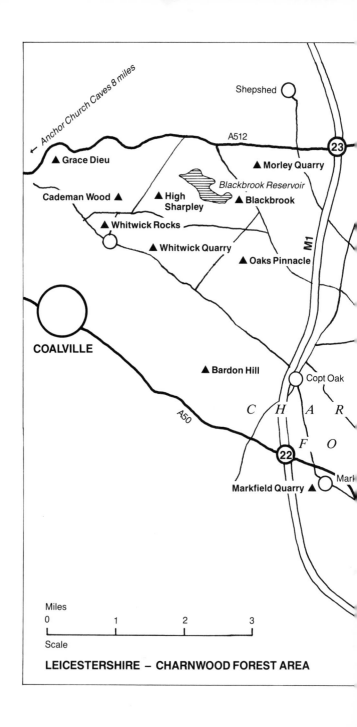

Anchor Church Caves 8 miles

Shepshed

A512

23

▲ Grace Dieu

▲ Morley Quarry

Blackbrook Reservoir

Cademan Wood ▲

▲ High
Sharpley

▲ Blackbrook

M1

▲ Whitwick Rocks

▲ Whitwick Quarry

▲ Oaks Pinnacle

COALVILLE

▲ Bardon Hill

Copt Oak

C   H   A   R

A50

F   O

22

Mark

Markfield Quarry ▲

Miles

0   1   2   3

Scale

LEICESTERSHIRE – CHARNWOOD FOREST AREA

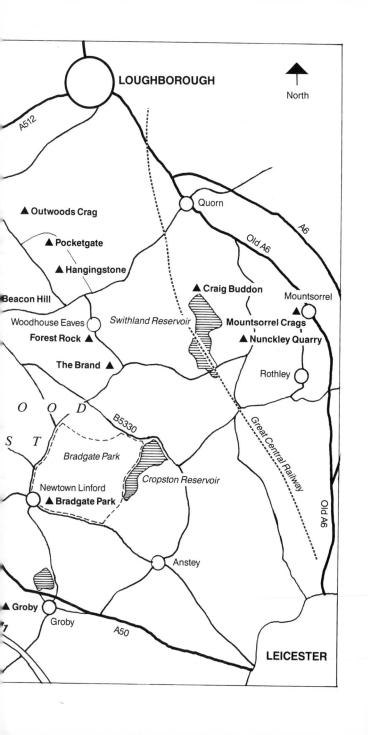

Greg Lucas on Saucy (E3), FOREST ROCK, Woodhouse Eaves.
Photo: I. Morris

LEICESTERSHIRE

CLIMBS

Geoff Mason
Ken Vickers

**Photographs
by
Greg Lucas**

CORDEE · LEICESTER

Previous guides:

1966 Rock Climbs in Leicestershire – Interim Guide, K.S. Vickers

1973 Climbs in Leicestershire, K.S. Vickers

First Edition: 1993

British Library Cataloguing in Publication Data
Mason Geoff., 1941–, Vickers Ken, 1941–

   Leicestershire Climbs
   1.Leicestershire.   Rock Climbing
   2.Leicestershire, Charnwood Forest.   Rock Climbing
   I.Title.
   796.5223094254

ISBN 1 871890 61 6

Distributed by CORDEE, 3a De Montfort Street, Leicester, LE1 7HD

Front cover: Steve Etherington on *Virago* E1 5a, Craig Buddon. Photo
              Tony Charles

Rear cover: the water-level traverse of *Baptism* VS 5b (4c variant),
             Markfield Quarry. Photo John Lockett

This guidebook has been written on a voluntary basis. 5% of the price is
contributed to the BMC Access and Conservation Fund, which campaigns
for access to, and conservation of, crags and mountains throughout Britain,
and to The Open Spaces Society, which campaigns to create and preserve
common land, village greens, open spaces and rights of public access.

Printed in Great Britain by BPCC Wheatons Ltd, Exeter

CONTENTS

INTRODUCTION

It is usually thought that there is little or no worthwhile climbing i Leicestershire. There are two reasons. The first is that there really isn a lot of climbing in Leicestershire and the second is that the guide boo to what there is has been out of print for many years.

In this time much has happened. The longer climbs are all in quarries t which the access is always changing; Huncote and Whitwick ar examples. Even worse, it has also become fashionable to fill them in, an quarries such as Enderby, Barrow Hill and the lower tier of Whitwick hav mostly disappeared. Even though a guidebook has been in preparatio for many years such external factors have kept undoing the work an preventing completion. Without the guidebook local knowledge has bee lost and once-popular crags have become overgrown and obscur boulders have been "lost".

A guidebook – any guidebook – has become an urgent need. And her it is. Speed has been of the essence and it is a collation of contribution of the many past editors over the years, but brought up to date and revise with as much current knowledge as can be gathered quickly.

There have been the usual discussions on what should be included an these have mainly been decided on the availability of information. Thi guide is not a comprehensive exposition on a developed area, merely holding operation.

THE ROCKS OF LEICESTERSHIRE

Leicestershire is a diverse county, geologically speaking. The doubl landscape of Leicestershire – lush smooth valley contrasting with the bar rugged uplands – is caused by very ancient mountains of hard (in physical, not climbing sense) old rock poking through the more-recent ma deposits. The upland soil is thin and poor and is frequently rough moorlan or old oakwood. Charnwood Forest was described by Burton in 1622 a "of hard barren soil, full of hills, woods, rocks of stone, tors and dells of kind of slate." Things have not changed much and the ancient summit still have small crags and tors set in areas of great scenic beauty. Howeve although the rock is good, the climbs are short, rarely being more tha boulder problems. But the hard rock has also been of use locally. Th walls of the fields and old houses are built from it. There are even slate on the roofs split from it. The places these useful stones originally cam from were the summits where the rocks were exposed. Sometimes th quarries ate deeply into the hill, but usually the summits, as at Bardon an Markfield, survived. Slate outcrops were followed downward into dee pits. The quarrying of the ancient hills has left a network of old quarrie and pits in the hard rock areas of the county.

So Leicestershire crags give bouldering on hilltops and in woods an longer routes in the old quarries.

There are two main rock types from the climbing viewpoint – slate an granite, and both occur as natural tors and as quarries. The natural tor of slate are usually in woods because the soil is too poor for much else The slate quarries are of modest scale, unlike North Wales, and quit frequently flooded. They are sometimes very deep. The granite als occurs as natural tors on some hills and almost every village has an old small quarry, most likely called Parish Pit. The later Victorian quarries were made possible by the cheap transport of the railways. They are generally big and intimidating. Leicestershire was producing over a million tons of granite a year by 1900. However, some quarries, such as Craig Buddon which produced stone for a dam, are modest and could almost pass as a natural crag. Recently the quarrying of stone has reached epidemic proportions and absolutely massive quarries, square miles in extent, and hundreds of feet deep have appeared. These new quarries have either eaten up the old quarries or filled them in with overburden from land freshly prepared for quarrying. None of the massive new quarries has yet been abandoned but it is obvious that just transporting the fill to refill them will be an enormous nuisance locally. With luck, they might survive and even leave some climbable rock.

The reason that Leicestershire has so many quarries is that there is no hard rock for roadstone etc. to the south-east. Leicester granite is the nearest (and thus cheapest) hard rock to London. Leicestershire produces 40% of the hard rock quarried in England, a vastly disproportionate share.

CRAG ORDER

The climbing is concentrated in the hard rock areas of Charnwood Forest and in a small area of hard intrusive rock south of Leicester.

There are many crags in this guide and putting them into an obvious order is difficult. The crags south of Leicester (mainly Huncote) form a natural group but the ones in Charnwood Forest (almost everything else) would then be an overlarge group.

The crags are listed in alphabetical order with a group of minor crags under M. This is not ideal, but it is as logical as anything else. Where a minor crag is near a major one, it is listed at the end of the section on the major crag. Crag locations can be roughly obtained from the area maps and detailed approach maps are usually given with the entry.

GRADING CLASSIFICATIONS

Much has been written on how to grade climbs. In this guide a combination of adjectival grades and technical grades is used. The system follows that currently used in the BMC Peak District guides. The sequence of adjectival grades is Moderate (M), Difficult (D), Very Difficult (VD), Severe (S), Hard Severe (HS), Very Severe (VS), Hard Very Severe (HVS) and Extremely Severe. The Extremely Severe grade is open ended; E1, E2, E3...... . Technical grades identify the technical difficulty of crux moves and the sequence is, in order of increasing difficulty, 3a, 3b, 3c, 4a, 4b, 4c, 5a, 5b, 5c, 6a, 6b, 6c, etc. Again, open ended.

ROUTE QUALITY

The system of stars, which has found wide acceptance, has been followed. There are three stars for the best routes and none for the worst. It should not be assumed that routes without stars are not worth doing. It is merely that they have no star quality. A negative scale (including black spots and daggers) is needed to identify the really unfortunate routes, but this has not been done here.

FIRST ASCENTS

Where information is available the first ascensionists together with the date of the first ascent have been recorded. Where there are several claimants for the same route the Editors have done their best (which wasn't much) to resolve the problem.

CRAG AND ROUTE NAMES

Some crag names have been changed, notably Granitethorpe (previously Sapcote Quarry), Whitwick Rocks (previously Peldar Tor) and Nunckley Quarry (previously Kinchley Hill Quarry). Sapcote Quarry is actually a different one to the climbing quarry and Peldar Tor is not in Whitwick but along the road towards Leicester.

Alternative names for crags have been given where these are known. Because of the complexity of its ancient Precambrian rocks, Leicestershire has a very rich geological literature. To relate the climbing crags to the rocks in this geological literature you have to know what the crags and quarries were once called. Carvers Rocks is a classic example. It is never mentioned under that name in the geological literature.

Some climbs have had multiple names because of several claimed "first" ascents and also because routes were renamed after aid was reduced. There is no perfect way of solving this problem and again the Editors have done their best (so keep arguing about it).

ACCESS

The major problem for climbers in Leicestershire is access. The county is in a time warp with various interests trying to exclude climbers. It's like the 30's. Even the public parks have not been without problems. But it is the quarries with their extensive rock exposures that do and will pose the greatest problem. The quarries are there to supply hard rock aggregate to the populous South East. But this also means that for climbers from the South East the Leicestershire quarries are the nearest crags. This fact does not help access but is a prediction of potential demand.

All land belongs to somebody (or some Company) and they are legally entitled to deny access.

THE INCLUSION OF A CRAG OR THE ROUTES UPON IT IN THIS GUIDEBOOK DOES NOT MEAN THAT ANY MEMBER OF THE PUBLIC HAS THE RIGHT OF ACCESS TO THE CRAG OR THE RIGHT TO CLIMB UPON IT.

So far the crags have been lightly used, and whilst a landowner may have tolerated infrequent visits by local people he may take a different view if the numbers increase substantially. Under the Occupiers Liability Act 1984 climbing is classified as a risk activity and the landowner has no liability towards climbers unless climbing is conducted as a business on the site (i.e. he charges). Under the most recent Mines and Quarries Act and the Health and Safety at Work Act there is a legal requirement for a quarry owner to exclude the public from his workings. There is no prospect, with current legislation, of the BMC negotiating access agreements to working quarries, even to disused faces.

CONSERVATION

Many of the crags in this guide are Sites of Special Scientific Interest (SSSI's) and restrictions are imposed on the landowner by English Nature on what can and can't be done. Other crags are in areas of natural beauty or public ownership. Then there are the quarries – but if they are old then even they are softened by the years. There is no reason why climbing and the conservation of such areas should not co-exist if the usual good manners of the countryside are complied with. So far the only problems in Leicestershire have been connected with the numbers of visitors to areas and climbers have been an infinitesimal part of these numbers. But with increased use this may not be the case, and climbers using the crags should try to minimise the effect of their passing. Where special restrictions apply they have been noted in the text.

CHIPPING, BOLTING AND PEGGING

Many of the routes in this guide have been put up with the minimum of fixed gear. It is hoped that the Bosch and dangle brigade will not deface classic crags with bolts and pegs. This applies particularly to Beacon Hill, Craig Buddon, Pocketgate Quarry and Hangingstone Quarry. Go to Morley Quarry if you must. Remember the words of Geoffrey Winthrop Young "Getting to the top is nothing; how you do it is everything". Even Slawston Bridge has its ethics. On the first ascent of the traverse of Pipe Wall a hold was chipped. When the route was subsequently done "clean" the offending pocket was filled with Tetrion (exterior grade, of course). Hence the name, *Tetrion Traverse*.

WARNING

This guidebook contains a lot of information. Whilst a reasonable effort has been made to ensure accuracy it is obvious that errors must be present. After all it is sixteen years since the last guide went out of print. So don't regard any information (and that includes the grades!) as gospel, treat it with circumspection.

NEW CRAGS and NEW ROUTES

If you find a new crag (it's been known), or make a new climb please send details, with dates (and these days, reliable witnesses) to Ken Vickers, CORDEE, 3a De Montfort Street, Leicester LE1 7HG. Details should also be written up in the New Routes Books which are held by Roger Turner Mountain Sports, 52 London Road, Leicester LE2 0QD and Canyon Mountain Sports, 92 Granby Street, Leicester LE1 1DS.

ACKNOWLEDGEMENTS

This guide owes most to the two previous Leicestershire guidebooks edited by Ken Vickers. Many people have helped in getting and checking the information in this volume; in particular:

S. Allen, F. Ball, J. Bates, A Blowers, C. Carrington, M. Chaney, J. Codling, B. Davis, I. Dring, S. Gutteridge, J. Hart, M. Hood, T. Johnson, D. Jump,

8   INTRODUCTION . . .

J. Lockett, G. Lucas, C. Maddocks, J. Mitchell, J. Moulding, S. Neal, R. Pillinger, R. Ramsbottom, A. Reynolds, C. Robinson, M. Sheldrake, P. Stidever, P. Wells and Bill Wright (BMC)

There must be others whose names have been lost from the various copies and rewrites of manuscripts. But getting the information is not all. It still needed word processing into the format of this guide. This was done by Gwen Massey and it is true to say that without her this guide would not have seen the light of day. Thanks, Gwen, for such a professional job and keeping cheerful through it all.   Thanks also to Loughborough University for the use of equipment and providing Library facilities.

An example of what has been lost. This is *Cacophany* in the old Enderby Quarry, taken in 1962, before the quarry was filled in. The groove on the right was never climbed and is now lost under 30m of rubbish and earth. This is Pete (Skully) Cross shortly before he fell off, pulled out all the micro-pegs, and hurt his back. He now lives in Australia.

CRAG QUALITY

As the number of climbs in the country has proliferated the idea of awarding stars for quality evolved so that the best climbs could be identified.

The system really needs extending to the crags themselves rather than the individual climbs. For example: how does Stanage compare with Lawrencefield? Or Cloggy with Dinas Bach? Or Stanage with Cloggy? Leicestershire needs such a system because the range of quality of the crags in this guidebook is enormous. The best crags are of national importance and the worst are insignificant rocks buried in overgrown woodland. In any assessment of crag quality it is obvious that the total length of climbing is important, as also is the star quality of the routes, together with atmosphere and pleasantness. One could discuss endlessly how to do this, just like grading routes and awarding stars. As a first effort (and it is quite good enough to assess the Leicestershire crags) we can award "points" based on the number and length of climbs together with their star quality. **Each metre of climbing on an ordinary no-star route counts one point. For a one-star route each metre counts two points, for a two-star route it counts three points, and for a three-star route each metre counts four points.**

When applied to the Peak District, a few selected crags give the following approximate scores

Stanage	15,000	points
Froggatt	3,000	points
Bamford	1,800	points
Black Rocks	1,530	points
Yarncliffe Q.	1,000	points
Mother Cap	40	points

For Leicestershire the list is as follows:

1 **Huncote Quarry** (2969 points). Was the best; *Numero Uno*; 45m of granite in an old quarry. Part of a working quarry and ECC are under a legal obligation to keep you out. Recently (Jan. 1993) part quarried away.

2 **Markfield Quarry** (1524 points). 72 routes of all grades in a fine situation in a disused granite quarry. Conveniently placed for access from the M1.

3 **The Brand** (707 points). Hard routes on slate in the garden of the ex-Lord Lieutenant of Leicestershire.

4 **Pocketgate Quarry** (616 points). A desperate lichenous slab of slate in an old quarry amongst the trees.

5 **Granitethorpe Quarry** (497 points). Climbs of all grades above a flooded pit.

6 **Bardon Hill** (460 points). A mountain atmosphere on Leicestershire's highest summit – but part of an active quarry. To be released soon? Scope for new routes. Many acres of rock.

7 **Hangingstone Quarry** (413 points). Superb hard routes in an old slate quarry.

8 **Craig Buddon** (397 points). A jewel. Fine, but unprotected, climbin on a beautifully-sited compact crag beside a reservoir. Gets evening su

9 **Beacon Hill** (376 points). Outcrop boulder problems in a fine situatio

10 **Carvers Rocks** (292 points). Soft sandstone with good landings.

11 **Slawston Bridge** (280 points). Desperate finger work on an ol railway bridge. The shortest approach walk in the U.K.

12 **Whitwick Quarry** (223 points). Fine routes remain above the fille and ruined premier climbing quarry of Leicestershire.

13 **Forest Rock** (203 points). Desperate slate climbing in a seclude shady quarry. One of the few sites to which there is legal access.

14 **Hangingstone Rocks** (181 points). Short climbs on fine rock in th middle of a private golf course.

15 **Anchor Church Caves** (149 points). Weird rock; good cave.

16 **Groby Industrial Estate** (144 points). Short climbs on the top remain of an old filled quarry with an industrial estate. Good steps on the wa down.

17 **Outwoods Crag** (138 points). Easy routes of character in the trees

18 **Blackbrook Reservoir** (102 points). Loose and getting wooded, bt a fine position.

19 **Whitwick Rocks** (72 points). Super rock behind a hostile garage now getting overgrown.

20 **Morley Quarry** (60 points). Scope for development but suicida finishes.

The obvious anomaly is that a brilliant, but underdeveloped, crag woul score zero points. In this guidebook Grace Dieu Viaduct (with a possibl 400 points) falls into this category. Bardon Hill is lowly rated because is so underdeveloped.

STOP PRESS

A recent visit revealed that **SHEET HEDGES QUARRY** (aroun SK526083), near Groby, looks as if it is about to be abandoned. Thi granite quarry has been worked from mid-Victorian days to the presen and contains much rock exposure, a lot in long continuous faces "Contains more rock than all of the rest of Leicestershire" has been said Hard to believe if you've ever seen Bardon Hill.

Further enquiries confirm that the quarry has reserves for only anothe three years. However, planning permission has been sought to quarr the causeway between the two pits. This is about 20 million tons an would extend the quarry life by 40 years. Because the application doe not seek to extend the boundary of the quarry it is likely, but not certain that permission will be granted.

HISTORY

Earliest reports of climbing in Leicestershire date from the nineteenth century. Ernest Baker and Kyndwr Club members scrambled on the limestone of Breedon Hill (see Moors, Crags and Caves, 1903). Not surprisingly, quarrying has since erased their efforts. Climbing must have taken place between the wars at Beacon Hill, Hangingstone Rocks and Pocketgate Quarry but no record exists. The first recorded routes still intact were the work of Peter Harding in 1945-46, who apparently climbed "all obvious lines" on Carvers Rocks and Anchor Church Caves, which must have included most of the existing routes up to VS. From 1949 to the middle 50's, Peter and Barrie Biven, and Trevor Peck were active, their most notable contribution being *Christ* (HVS,5a, now E1, 5b) on Hangingstone Quarry in 1954, together with several classic problems at Beacon Hill, Hangingstone Rocks, Bardon Quarry, and Bradgate Park.

By 1959 Ken Vickers and Dave Draper had arrived on the scene. They formed the nucleus of the Leicester Association of Mountaineers, and were responsible for discovering and developing a number of crags, among them being Craig Buddon, Markfield Quarry and Whitwick Quarry and the Sixties were greeted with a steady flow of new routes from them and their friends. These included the classic *Virago* (VS, now E1) on Craig Buddon, and the first routes on Whitwick and Enderby Quarries. By the time the 1966 guidebook came out The Brand and Huncote Quarry were established on the climbers' map, and Hangingstone Quarry sported the area's first Extreme in *Christ Almighty*, albeit with some doubt about the amount of aid employed.

Several names came to the fore after publication of the guide including David Cooper, Chris Burgess, David Holyoak, John Gale, Godfrey Boulton and Roger Withers. Some were members of what had become the Leicester Mountaineering Club, and all were keen on unearthing new routes, sometimes literally. 1968 saw the ascent of *Red Wall Arête* (HVS, now gone) at Whitwick, and a year later John Harwood freeclimbed the technical *Stretcher* (HVS) at Huncote, then the most important climbing ground in Leicestershire. Also at Huncote, David Cooper created the excellent *Little Nightmare* (HVS now E1) and the immense *Girdle Traverse* (HVS), as well as many routes of lesser quality. The early Seventies saw no great steps forward in difficulty, with possible exception of *Trespass* (E1,5c, now gone) at Whitwick, a fierce problem which rated HVS in Ken Vickers' 1973 guide. In the realm of bouldering, however, the Slawston Bridge era had arrived, giving the next generation of climbers a material advantage in training facilities. The hardest problem here at the time was an eliminate on the Pipe Wall by Chris Hunter, still rated hard for 6a.

From 1977 a group of Leicester University climbers became the driving force, headed by John Moulding and Paul Mitchell. Partnered by various combinations of Bob Conley, Stephen Boothroyd, Fred Stevenson and Peter Wells, their campaign opened on Whitwick Quarry, which received a number of new routes. Notable were *Mr. Kipling's Country Slice* (E1,5b, now gone), *Freebird* (E2,5c, now gone), a spectacular free version of *The Nuts*, and *Born To Be Wild* (E3,6a, now gone), a very sustained crack line. Sadly, all these were on the now-buried lower tier. Huncote gave its share of the action in *Heat Treatment* (E2,5b), based loosely on the old *Rack Direct*, and *The Crimp* (E3,6a,5c) climbed without recourse to aid. Hangingstone Quarry became a minor forcing ground, with routes such as *Weekend Warrior* (E3,5b), *Christ Almighty* free (E2,5c), and the superb *Old Rock'n'Roller* (E2,5c), the free version of *Cloiste Groove*. Moulding managed a flawed lead of *Sheer Heart Attack* (E4,6a) using the only protection peg as a toehold. Nevertheless, this remained for some time the hardest route in the county, and is still regarded as a testpiece with a recent bolt for protection. It is interesting to speculate on the origins of *Holy Ghost* (E3,5c) given its ancient lineage and old grade of HVS.

Also involved with development during this period were Steve Gutteridge and Simon Pollard, both of the Leicester Bowline Club. Pollard freed *Three Peg Wall* (E1,6a) on Carver's Rocks and *Sorcerer* (E1,5b) on Forest Rock, while Gutteridge created, amongst other things, the immaculate *Starship Trooper* (6a) on Beacon Hill. Slawston Bridge stayed ahead in the technical stakes with the Pipe Wall traverse at 6b/c.

In 1981, Steve Allen and John Codling ushered in the modern era, and within two years had accounted for most of the obvious challenges. Climbing together and sharing leads, they were responsible for first ascents, or first free ascents, of the following routes: *Modular* (E4,6b) on The Brand, formerly A1; *Arrows of Desire* at Markfield (E3, 6a); the extremely strenuous *Sorcerer's Apprentice* (E4,6b) on Forest Rock; *Catchpenny Twist* (E3,5c, now gone) – a free climb based on *The Plague*, *Tumble Trier* (E3,5c, now gone) and *Pagan* (E4,6b, now gone), all on Whitwick, and a stream of high quality lines in Huncote Quarry. These include *Firing Squad* (E4,5c), *Eton Rifles* (E4,6b), *Intensive Scare* (E4,6a) and the desperate *Steeleye Span* (E4,6b/c). Allen and Codling were probably the first climbers to place protection bolts in Leicestershire, at least partly because *in situ* pegs were prone to disappearance.

And so to the future. Despite access problems and the steady encroachment by commercial interests on the remaining climbable rock, new routes continue to appear. The working quarries are producing acres of new rock but unfortunately modern blasting techniques shatter the rock more than the older methods, leaving a less suitable medium for climbing in the immediate future. This probably means that recently closed quarries may provide scope only for the truly dedicated. However, some classic crags must inevitably remain untouched by quarrying and Slawston Bridge will hopefully resist weathering well into the next century – but maybe the Council will straighten the bend in the road.

ANCHOR CHURCH CAVES

ANCHOR CHURCH CAVES

OS ref. SK339273
(Sheet 128)

SITUATION and CHARACTER

Anchor Church Caves are beside the Old River Trent near Ingleby. There is a public footpath at the bottom of the crag – or at the top when the river floods in winter. The crag is over 100m long and up to 12m high and in a very attractive setting. The main feature is not the crag at all, but the Hermit's Cave (an anchorite is a hermit). This cave has been cut from the rock (its that soft) and is complete with door openings and window holes. It is very unusual. The local kids use it as a playground and the fishermen use it as a place to get warm. The cliff is worth a visit just to see the cave. The cave is very old, being mentioned first in 1648. The Old River Trent has an interesting history. The course of the river was altered artificially so that 300 acres changed sides (Shakespeare, Henry IV, Pt.i., Act III, Sc. 1).

The rock is unfortunate. It is Triassic conglomerate, which is a sediment with protruding beds of pebbles. If the pebbles stick out far enough to be useful as holds then they are likely to come out. This adds real excitement, and those of a nervous disposition use top ropes. There are plenty of trees at the top for belays. The crag has an open aspect and faces north.

Peter Harding climbed here in 1945-47 whilst he was at Loughborough College, presumably because he didn't have enough petrol to go anywhere decent. The crag is not in Leicestershire at all, but is included here because no other guide would want it.

APPROACH and ACCESS

The best approach is from Ingleby (near the famous old Swarkestone Bridge across the Trent) along the public footpath which runs along the top of a steep bank before dipping down to the river and the Caves. Alternatively one can approach from the other end of the path which starts near Foremark, part of Repton School. It takes about 10 minutes from either end to get to the Caves. There has been no problem with access.

THE CLIMBS

Due to the rock, gradings given here are suspect, especially in the E grades. All the routes are serious because no protection can be placed. The climbs are described from left to right.

1 **A Pebble Too Far**   8m   E1   5c
Direct over the largest part of the overhang to a decaying tree root a few feet left of *Monks Folly*. *D. Jump, 1989.*

2 **Monks Folly**   8m   E1   5c
The overhanging wall on the far left-hand end of the crag can be climbed by a line ascending leftwards to a tree.

3. **Close Shave**   10m   HVS   5a
The arête to the left of the first window, trending left to the tree. *P. Stidever.*

4 **Pillar of Wisdom**   10m   S
Climbs the main rounded arête starting at either side of the window. *M. Sheldrake and M. Hood, March 1981.*

5 Hermit's Crack   10m   VS   4b
The obvious groove in the back of the cliff.

6 The Ramp   10m   VS   4b
Start in *Hermit's Crack* but trend rightwards up the obvious ramp. Serious.

7 Pebble Dash   12m   E2   5b
Start just left of the left window on the front face. Climb the wall direct.

8 Hermit's Finger   12m   E2   5a
Climb the crack line between the two caves.

9 PS170   12m   HVS   5a
Starts to the right of the window, climbing past a pocket then trending left.
Maybe harder than HVS. *P. Stidever and M. James.*

10 Monkey Business   12m   VS   4c
The arête just left of the cave. Maybe harder than VS. *M. James.*

11 Doorway   10m   not done
Bridge up the doorway and go up over a small roof.

Don't forget the Girdle (1-11) above the nettles!

Twenty metres to the right there is some clean rock with three obvious pockets at the bottom. These may have been cut to secure a fence.

12 New Boots – New Routes   10m   VS   4c
Climbs the face to the right of three obvious pockets, then up a flake to finish. Overgrown. *M. James.*

13 Pete's Progress   10m   D
The obvious large chimney at the right-hand end of the crag. *M. James.*

Twenty metres further to the right there is:

14 Sandy Chimney   15m   M
Follow the right-hand branch of the obvious split chimney all the way up to the top. At the bottom there is a left-hand branch also.

Further along a ramp leads up behind some trees to a fierce overhanging upper tier. No routes here yet. Nor on the right arête. Much further right is a small cave, the right wall of which has possibilities.

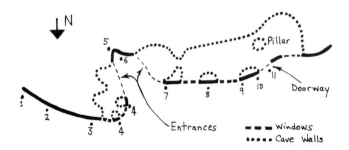

BARDON HILL

OS ref. SK459132
(Sheet 129)

SITUATION and CHARACTER

The highest point in Leicestershire (278m) looks over an enormous quarry, the source of a greenish crystalline rock, the much-prized Bardon "good rock". The hill offers bouldering below the summit, an ancient quarried face, and who-knows-what on the slabs in the quarry. Currently (May 1992) the quarry north of the hill (Siberia) is being filled with overburden so that rock south of the hill can be extracted. It should take about 4 years to fill and the final level is uncertain. Climbs on the old quarry face at the top of the hill will probably survive, which is good because they have a mountain touch about them. They are exposed to the weather yet, facing west, they get a lot of summer sun. The summit is a wonderful place (if you can ignore the quarry and the radio masts). It has been claimed that the hill "commands a greater extent of surface than any other point of view in the island .... like an ocean view from a ship out of sight of land". You can see the Sugar Loaf in South Wales, the Shropshire Hills, and summits in N. Wales and Derbyshire.

The rock is a kind of granite. It was being quarried in 1622 and a small quarry is shown on the map of 1835. Large scale working started in 1857 and the quarry is described as "great" by 1877. By 1890 it had been "much enlarged" and was working at three levels. The summit quarry probably dates from this period. Certainly the face was there in 1910 as it is shown on old maps. The quarrying technique was interesting. Four inch holes were drilled and then "sprung" with successive small charges until a chamber was formed sufficient for the main charge of explosive. This could be as much as 15cwt (750kg). Almost all the rock went for roadstone or railway ballast. The man responsible for the quarry was Breedon Everard who worked the little quarry at Billa Barra and lived in Bardon Hall. He had a summer house on the summit of Bardon Hill. He went on to form Ellis and Everard, a Leicestershire supplier of builders' materials.

APPROACH and ACCESS

The summit of Bardon Hill is the most remote crag in this guide. There are three approaches:

1. From the Copt Oak-Whitwick Road (B587) take the first left after leaving Copt Oak (1.5 miles) towards the Agar Nook estate. Take the first left (Romans Crescent) and park near Vercor Close (yes, it's true). A footpath starts from Vercor Close and leads round the Siberia quarry to the private road leading to the summit of Bardon Hill. It is worth walking up to the rim to look into the defile of the quarry – the Grand Canyon of Leicestershire – while it is still there.

2. Take a footpath off the Copt Oak-Whitwick road about half a mile from Copt Oak, past Kellam's Farm and on to the private road that leads to the radio masts on the top of Bardon Hill.

3. Start from the A50, near an old chapel (469116) and take the footpath past Old Rise Rocks farm (some spectacular outcrops but no climbing) and continue to the summit.

The radio masts are a couple of hundred metres east of the trig point and various little paths link the two. The climbing is directly below the trig point. A secure wire fence bars access by the summit but the fence is not so secure in the wood to the south. It should be possible to scramble down to the platform below the climbs, alternatively abseil. It is possible to get onto a lower terrace about 500m east of the summit (there's a hole in the fence beside the road) and walk along below slabs etc. to the climbing area.

Because of the possibility of stonefall it would be hazardous to attempt to climb whilst the men filling the quarry are working below.

Access has been restricted and the quarry is possibly covered by the Mines and Quarries Act. However, as filling proceeds, it is likely that more of Bardon Hill will become an area to which the public has access and these routes (and more) will become available again. There is no information from anyone who has recently climbed at Bardon but visitors all agree that there is much scope for new routes on the slabs and buttresses on the top tiers of the Siberia quarry. The quarry is owned by Bardon Hill Quarries.

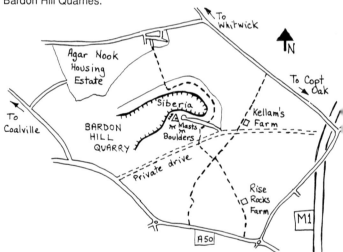

BARDON HILL QUARRY

THE CLIMBS

The climbs are taken from the old guide book with little revision. First ascents date back to Biven and Peck in the forties and early fifties. The routes are described from left to right. All but one start on the top terrace.

1 Funky Dudes   42m   VD
Above the centre of the left-hand terrace is an obvious corner crack.
1.   24m. Climb the crack to a large grass ledge and belay well back on a tree below another crack.
2.   18m. Up the crack past two smaller trees and a grass ledge to regain rock at the summit. *B. McGaw, D. Morgan and A. Crofts, Oct. 1978.*

2 Silava Slabs   30m   D
From the middle of the left-hand terrace an obvious pavement of slabs can be seen leading up to the right. Follow it.

3 The Flake   30m   VD
Start at the far right of the left-hand terrace.
1.   6m. Up over a short wall to a large ledge.
2. 18m. From the centre of the ledge climb a short steep wall mantle-shelfing into a groove which leads to The Flake. Climb it to a large stance and belay.
3. 12m. Make off to the left over easier ground to the top.

4 Zig-Zag   45m   VS
Start from the left end of the right-hand terrace.
1.   9m. Traverse horizontally left to make an interesting step into a large grassy corner.
2.   6m. Ascend the finger crack until an awkward move left can be made to another corner.
3. 21m. Climb the corner crack to terrace. Ascend the flake crack to a large stance and belay.
4.   9m. Take the small overhang behind the block belay by a few trying moves and get on to easy slabs.

5 Underhand   39m   VS
1. 15m. Start from the right-hand terrace below the centre of the large overhang. Move left up under the overhang and to the top of a pyramid shaped block. Climb up on to a large ledge.
2. 15m. Ascend the second overhang by the slight but obvious break.
3.   9m. Up over easy ground to the top.

6 Pigeon Cleft   39m   VD
1.   9m. Start to the right of the large overhang. Scramble up rightwards into the large grassy rake. Block belay.
2. 15m. Make a move left over straightforward ground to a stance and flake belay.
3. 15m. Move up and left into the Cleft. Follow it and easier ground to the top.

7 Black Cleft   37m   S
1.   7m. Start from the terrace below a stunted birch. Climb up to the left; a little loose at the top. Belay to a block in the rake.
2. 15m. Ascend easy rocks to narrow terrace. Make an interesting move right from the top of a block on to a large ledge below the prominent Black Cleft.
3. 15m. Climb the groove, awkward to enter, and belay a little back from the edge. Possibly the best route at Bardon.

HS variant. From the left of a large ledge below the Cleft climb a groove to the base of the wall then move out left and over the wall by good holds.

8 Primo Crack   34m   D
1.   7m. As for *Black Cleft.*
2. 27m. Walk up the rake for 7m to below the obvious crack leading to the top. Climb directly up. A belay can be arranged half way.

9   **Birch Tree Rib**   27m   VD

9tart from the terrace. Climb a prominent rib with large birch tree half way up. It can be very greasy and some of the holds are not too sound.

10   **Girdle Traverse**   100m   VS

On the whole an interesting climb. Nearly all is climbing done on fresh ground. Start as far left as possible by the large grassy bank on the first tier level (Peg belay).

1. 21m. Traverse along the obvious foot ledge onto the left-hand terrace. Walk to the end. Peg belay. (Loose).

2. 11m. Move across the wall and make an awkward move into an overleaning corner, peg runner by the feet. Make another very awkward step around onto the large grassy stance and peg belay of *Zig-Zag*.

3. 9m. Up the finger crack of *Zig-Zag*, keeping straight on – nut belays.

4. 20m. Traverse right along the broken wall by a large grassy slab to the block belay of *Pigeon Cleft*.

5. 15m. Move across the slab. Step down onto the wall to a small sapling (runner). Step down again onto the slab and move across to belay on the smaller and higher of the two trees on Birch Tree Rib. Good pitch.

6. 24m. Step down and round the corner onto the steep wall on good holds and traverse across with interest on gradually deteriorating rock. From here one can move up and aim for one of the belays on the top.

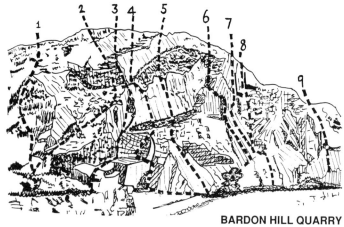

BARDON HILL QUARRY

On the next tier down and beneath The Flake *a large slab slopes up to the right at about 60˚. This gives:*

11   **Friction Grip**   37m   S   4a

Start in the middle of the slab and climb straight up to the grassy terrace at the top. The slab bulges slightly at about 25m. Positive holds are few and protection non-existent. *J. Cooil and M. Williams, 12 July 1975.*

BARDON HILL BOULDERS

On the top of the hill to the south of the ridge between the trig point and the radio mast are a number of small outcrops on which problems can be found. They face south and lie in the relatively clear area above the trees. Nice on a summer afternoon.

BEACON HILL

OS ref. SK508149
(Sheet 129)

SITUATION and CHARACTER

At 248m Beacon Hill is the second highest point in Leicestershire and, hardly surprisingly, commands a wonderful view. The Soar and Trent valleys sweep around the northern panorama and Charnwood Forest and Leicester lie to the south. You can see the spire of Lincoln cathedral on a clear day. The area is an important public open-country recreation area and can get quite crowded with visitors walking, flying kites and exercising dogs. The crag tops have been polished by the passage of thousands of feet. But it does mean that it is one of the few crags with a public toilet and ice cream van.

The rocks offer bouldering but some of the longer routes are a bit too high to fall off with impunity. Some landings are dangerous. The summit crags are exposed and can be cold on a windy day. The rock is Beacon Hill Hornstone – another Precambrian sedimentary rock formed from ancient volcanic ash. It weathers in some places to become white and creamy and polishes easily, when it becomes slippery. The bedding planes dip to the north and the exposed faces laminate off. The slaty blades give rise to the abrupt arêtes, pinnacles and blocks that are so typical of the Charnwood outcrops. They have huge jugs and also smooth sloping holds. The Beacon outcrops have not been quarried and, despite their open aspect, can be green and very slippery when wet. The routes are generally steep gymnastic problems.

APPROACH and ACCESS

From Junction 22 on the M1 take the A50 towards Burton-on-Trent for 3/4 mile to the first roundabout. Turn right along the B591 towards Copt Oak. Turn off right after 2 miles, still following the B591, and the Beacon top car park is signposted on the left after another two miles. The keeper shuts the gate promptly at the time indicated by the sign, so take care and do not get locked in.

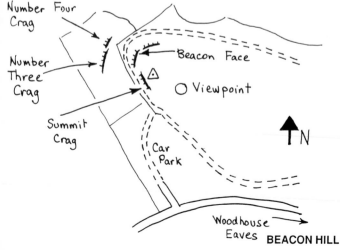

The area is managed by the Bradgate Trust as a recreation area. There have been few problems with access. The warden has been known to say that climbing is forbidden but the Bye-Laws displayed on the notice boards say no such thing.

THE CLIMBS

The first outcrop is **SUMMIT CRAG**, just to the south of the trig point, beside the track behind the wall. It is visible from the top car park. The rock is almost white and get the full sun.

There is an obvious overhang above some big boulders one of which forms a fine little pinnacle. From right to left are:

1 **Prop**   5m   VD
Mantleshelf up just to the right of the overhang.

2 **Auto**   5m   HVS   5a   *
Climb up to beneath the overhang, above the small pinnacle. Step right onto a large hold, back left, and then straight up.

3 **And You and I**   5m   E2   6a   **
Makes the move that *Auto* avoids. Climb left of the large hold on *Auto* straight over the overhang with a long reach from an undercut to gain a very small flake. Don't fall off; a hospital job awaits! *S. Gutteridge, 1977.*

4 **Is There a Better Way**   5m   S   4a
Start directly behind the pinnacle. Swing right over the overhang and muscle up.

5 **Marine**   5m   D
Start about 2m left of the little pinnacle. Straight up the lower and upper walls on big jugs.

6 **Fire**   5m   S   4a
Just left of *Marine* is a steep polished little wall. Skate up the first moves and scramble to the top.

7 **Shaft**   5m   D
5m left of the little pinnacle. Climb a rib and continue. Almost a continuous route.

Following the track north-westerly down and round the summit for 50m leads to **THE BEACON FACE**, so called because of the profile of a head can be seen from some directions. There are two climbing sections with a broken section between. The routes on the right-hand section from right to left, are:

8 **Outside Wall**   5m   S   4a
Start just right of the large boulder by the obvious V gully. Climb the well-scratched wall on big holds without using the boulder.

9 **Right Arête**   6m   HVS   5a
Climb the right arête of the V gully, either direct or from the boulder or by traversing out of the gully.

10 **Circus of Heaven**   6m   E1   5c   *
Climb the right wall of the V gully without using the arête or boulder. *S. Gutteridge.*

11 **V Gully**   6m   VS   4b   **
Climb the V gully direct. A deceptive undertaking. Graded Severe in the old guide when it had an extra hold. If all else fails, turn round and face out.

12 **Moonshot Direct**   6m   E1   6a
The left wall of the V gully direct. Use layaways to reach the polished jugs then mantleshelf and layback using a poor high flake directly above for the left hand. *S. Gutteridge.*

13 **Moonshot**   6m   E1   5b   ***
Start under the overhang on the left wall of the V gully. Reach for polished jugs by underclings and use a pinch layaway for the left hand to reach the obvious triangular hole up and to the left. Then straight up. In 1978 Steve Gutteridge and Pete Meads had a bit of a competition whenever either of them visited the Beacon. This eventually resulted in Pete doing 21 ascents of *Moonshot* (some of them by the *Direct*) in 18 minutes! No wonder it's polished.

14 **On the Silent Wings of Freedom**   6m   E2   6a
Start just left of *Moonshot* under the overhangs, swing out on undercut holds to make a hard move out onto the face. *S. Gutteridge.*

15 **Slippery Slabs**   5m   VD
Climb up 3m left of *Moonshot* on good holds.

15m further left a group of overhangs with a smooth slab below gives the next cluster of routes. Routes are listed from right to left. To the right of its right edge is:

16 **Nostril**   6m   VD
Just right of the aréte is a diamond-shaped overhang (the nose on the face of Beacon Face) above a little corner. Start up the rib to the right. Finish up the top wall by monster steps. Alternatively finish up the steep corner to the right.

17 **Left Nostril**   6m   VD
Climb the arête with a big step in the little corner, then follow the arête above. The other nostril.

18 **Right Corner**   5m   VD
Climb the corner at the right-hand end of the overhangs to a step up to the right around the overhang. Has an incredibly polished sloping hold and an excellent slot.

19 **Hot Rails to Hell**   5m   HVS   5a
Left of *Right Corner* lies a small corner. Climb the left face.

20 **Death Valley Nights**   5m   HVS   5a
Also called *Bimbo*. Climb the groove through the overhangs to the left of *Hot Rails to Hell* to finish direct over a small overhang at the top. *G. Rowley, Aug. 1980.*

21 **Limbo**   5m   VS   4c   *
Left of *Death Valley Nights* a short crack leads to the overhang. Climb this and the overhang above. *B.M. and P.H. Biven, 1957.*

22 **To Be Over**   5m   E1   5c   **
Climb the overhang to the left of *Limbo* from a recess. *S. Gutteridge.*

23 **Balsoon**   5m   HVS   5a   *
Climb the overhang direct at the left-hand end. *S. Gutteridge.*

The crag to the left is more broken with a slab topped by a line of overhangs.
There are several one-move middle-grade problems over the overhangs.
Because of the position they are exposed and not good to fall from.

**Greg Lucas on Starship Trooper (E1),
NUMBER THREE CRAG, Beacon Hill**

*The next two crags lie 150m down the hill to the west. Cross the track
and follow any path through the wall. The crags can also be reached
directly from the car park by taking a path to the north west across rough
ground between the two walls. The crags are in two groups. The most*

southerly is **NUMBER THREE CRAG** *which has a pair of obvious clean buttresses on either side of a deep gash. Routes are described from left to right.*

24 **Starship Trooper** 7m E1 6a ***
Ascend the overhanging arête left of the obvious crack/corner line. *S. Gutteridge, 7 July 1977.*

25 **Collywobble Crack** 7m HS 4b *
Climb the polished crack in the gash. Another deceptive undertaking.

26 **Third Time Lucky** 7m E1 5c **
Climb the middle of the wall right of the crack direct. No using the crack.

27 **The Last Straw** 7m HS 4b *
Step right onto the arête right of *Collywobble Crack*, and ascend. *B.M. and P.H. Biven, 1957.*

28 **Relayer** 7m E1 5c
Climb the wall right of the arête direct. *S. Gutteridge, 24 June 1977.*

29 **Ten Pin Wall** 7m HS 4b
Climb the wall by starting in the gully to reach a high hold and delicately layaway to finish at the top of the left arête.

30 **The Gully** 10m D
Climb the obvious gully.

31 **The Camel's Back** 10m HVS 5a
Climb the arête of the gully starting from the left.

32 **The Heart of the Sunrise** 10m E1 5c *
The front face of the arête, gained from the left. *S. Gutteridge.*

33 **Starlight** 10m HS 4b
Climb the crack right of the arête direct.

34 **Forest Wall** 10m VD
1m right of the crack. Up and left to the top.

35 **Forest Slabs** 10m D
The slabs give two obvious routes.

The fourth crag, **NUMBER FOUR CRAG,** *lies 20m to the north and has a small face with an obvious crack to the left.*

36 **Jack in the Box** 5m HS 4b *
Climb the obvious crack to gain a ledge on the left.

37 **Silk and Satin** 6m HVS 5c **
Climb the overhanging wall on the right direct. Utterly desperate.

38 **Bow** 4m VD **
Climb the overhanging arête to the right.

There is another crag 40m to the north but closer inspection reveals a heap of boulders which give few routes.

SUMMIT CRAG
Beacon Hill

1 D Shaft
2 S Fire
3 D Marine
4 S Is There a Better Way
5 E3 And You and I
6 HVS Auto
7 VD Prop

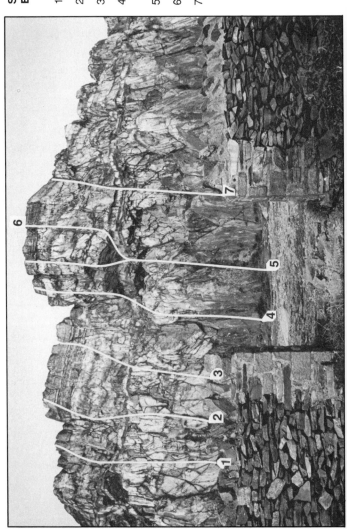

**THE BEACON FACE
RIGHT
Beacon Hill**

1	VD	Nostril
2	VD	Slippery Slabs
3	E2	On the Silent Wings of Freedom
4	E1	Moonshot
5	E1	Moonshot Direct
6	VS	V Gully
7	HVS	Right Arête
8	S	Outside Wall

THE BEACON FACE
LEFT
Beacon Hill

1   HVS   Balsoon
2   E1   To Be Over
3   VS   Limbo
4   HVS   Death Valley Nights
5   HVS   Hot Rails to Hell
6   VD   Right Corner
7   VD   Left Nostril
8   VD   Nostril

NUMBER THREE CRAG
Beacon Hill

1 E1 Starship
Trooper
2 HS The Last
Straw
3 E1 Relayer
4 E1 The Heart of
the Sunrise
5 HS Starlight
6 D Forest Slabs

NUMBER FOUR CRAG
Beacon Hill

1   HS   Jack in the Box
2   HVS   Silk and Satin
3   VD   Bow

BLACKBROOK RESERVOIR

OS ref. SK464171
(Sheet 129)

SITUATION and CHARACTER

More properly called One Barrow Plantation, this crag is an old granite quarry which was opened for the construction of the concrete dam across Blackbrook about the turn of the century. The dam replaced one built for the Loughborough to Ashby canal which collapsed in 1807, closing the canal. When the new dam was finished in 1906 it was damaged by an earthquake but the damage was deemed minor and the valley was flooded by Loughborough Corporation Waterworks.

The rock is the most ancient of the Precambrian rocks of Charnwood and has been much altered over time A geological fault passes close by the crag which may account for its preponderance to fall down. The crag is in a fine south-facing situation above the water at the east end of Blackbrook reservoir. Trees have grown up and the rock is in danger of disappearing. The rock (not the vegetation) is an SSSI.

The crag consists of strange red slabs, short steep bounding walls and overhangs. The main slab is stepped with small overhangs which detach from time to time. It was once thought that, with traffic, the crag would clean up. But there have been too many rockfalls for that to be believed now. The rock shatters into small pieces and has built up a useful talus slope at the bottom.

Because the water level in the reservoir goes up and down, more or less of the slope at the bottom is exposed. Even at "high water" the crag is accessible. At very low water there is some good additional climbing on the wall to the left of the main crag (another *Baptism*).

APPROACH and ACCESS

From interchange 23 on the M1 head west along the A512. Turn left at the second traffic lights (towards Oaks in Charnwood) and turn right at the cross-roads at the bottom of a hill. After about a quarter of a mile a small lane goes off to the left beside a house (Botany Bay). A few hundred yards down the lane one comes to the water and a magnificent over-engineered blue brick bridge which carries a track over to One Barrow Lodge. There is very limited parking here. It is best to park on the road at Botany Bay and walk down.

The crag is owned by Severn Trent who are very concerned about vandalism, less so about swimming (there are notices, so it is obviously a good spot), and hardly at all about climbing. The land at the top of the crag is owned by DeLisle, and the gamekeeper of High Sharpley has been known to try to turn people off.

THE CLIMBS

The quarry is a small watery bay cut into the hillside. At the very far left is a wall which gives an exciting traverse (*the Bigger Splash*, 4c, *D. Jump and S. Metcalf, Oct. 1976*). Probably better when the water level is down.

At the far left of the crag there is a bay at a higher level than the bottom of the main slab. There is a large holly tree growing out of the crag here.

To the left there is an excellent steep smooth red wall that will provide hard route or two.

Then there is:

1 **Fracas**   7m   VD
Start at the bottom of a well-defined corner to the left of the large ho tree. Layback up the rusty corner to the top.

2 **Hullabaloo**   15m   VD
The main slab is divided by a number of trees. Start on the left side of t left section 5m right of a holly bush. Climb straight up to a small tree a scramble up to the rock wall. Move right and ascend with caution. Bel on the top (30m from ground).

3 **Nameless**   30m   VS   4b
A route has been made right of *Hullabaloo* but no description, only t grade, is available. Presumably it goes over the overlaps.

4 **Red Slab**   20m   S
Start at a pine tree in the centre of the lowest part of the right hand secti (to the right of a recent rock fall). Move over a short wall then asce bearing slightly right to finish under the leaning blocks. Climb them w care going right, and move over loose ground for an extra 10m to bel on the top.

5 **Delicardo**   15m   S
Start 5m right of *Red Slab*. Straight up for 3m and then wander acro the slab to the right to escape from the leaning blocks. Finish at the right-hand corner.

6. **Easy Slab**   15m   D
The slab to the right of the main face can be scrambled on. Nothing abo Diff.

At the north end of the reservoir is a small overgrown quarry (45718 which might give a few routes (but probably won't).

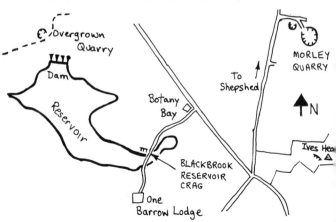

BLACKBROOK, IVES HEAD and MORLEY QUARR

BRADGATE PARK

About OS ref. SK526101
(Sheet 129)

SITUATION and CHARACTER

Situated four miles north west of Leicester, Bradgate Park is an ancient deer park given to the people of Leicestershire by Charles Bennion (a director of British United Shoe Company) in 1928 for their quiet recreation. Bradgate is a beautiful area of rolling bracken covered hills, walled spinneys, and small craggy outcrops of slate and granite. There are many ancient hollow oak trees, reputedly topped after the execution of Lady Jane Grey. The park is justifiably popular with visitors, so it is best avoided on Sundays and especially Bank Holidays.

Conspicuous from all over Leicestershire is the distinctive beer-mug shaped folly of Old John on the top of the highest hill. This is an 18th century observation tower built to give the ladies a view of a race course which circled the top of the hill. You can see the large stones marking the course circling the hill. The "handle" was built later to turn the tower into a beer-mug in memory, so the story goes, of a beer-loving family retainer who was killed when a pole in the middle of a bonfire burned through and fell on him. Believe that and you'll believe anything. Below the tower is the remains of a walled enclosure built into the rock face which was formerly a stable for the horses. There are one or two easy routes here. Below the War Memorial there are easy-angled crags, the haunt of children trying their first scrambles. These rocks are slaty and contain the ancient *Charniodiscus* fossil (see also Pocketgate Quarry).

APPROACH and ACCESS

There are three entrances to the Park which have car parks. The busiest is beside the church in Newtown Linford. There is a north entrance giving access to the Old John area and another way in on the east side near Cropston reservoir.

Activities in the Park are managed by County Hall and have been increasingly restricted in recent times. Climbing on the rocks is not actually forbidden by the displayed Bye Laws – although climbing the trees, walls and buildings is. The warden has been known to say that climbing is forbidden after the volume of public complaints (another Bye Law says you can't do anything that produces complaints).

THE CLIMBS

From the main entrance at Newtown Linford follow the surfaced track for 300m alongside the river Lin through Little Matlock Gorge. Situated high on the left above the track is a small crag behind the trees and to the left of some prominent, more broken, rocks. This is the **WISHING-STONE CRAG** (526100). It is Markfieldite granite and about 6m high. Much better than you might think.

1 **Thumbscrew**   4b   The thin crack from the left. *B.M. and P.H. Biven, 1949.*

2 **The Stretcher**   5c   Climb the wall direct.

3 **The Rack**   5a   Climb the wall just left of the arête.

4 **Cenotaph Corner**   4a   Compellingly obvious!

5 **Cemetery Gates**   4b   Climb the right arête, using the crack to start

Below and to the right is a good boulder with an arête and overhanging wall.

WISHING-STONE CRAG, Bradgate Park

Continue along the surfaced track for 800m until beside the ruins of Bradgate House. (Built for the Grey's of Groby in 1440 and home of Lady Jane Grey, the famous nine day Queen of England in 1553, burnt 1690). Turn right off the track and cross the river by a stone bridge. Behind the small rocky hillock in front of you, and invisible as you approach, is a small quarry. This is **STABLE PIT** *named after the stable block which was demolished in the 1850's, OS ref SK 534100 (its on the join of sheets 129 and 140). The rock is slate quartzite. The pit faces south and is relatively secluded.*

From the left-hand end of the wall:

6 **Thin Ragged Crack Slanting Left**   4c   Harder than it looks.

7 **Yours Is No Disgrace** 5c Climb the overhanging wall just left of the highest point of the crag (its only 4m), finishing over it.

8 **Tootal** 5a Just left of a round scoop at waist level to the gap right of the highpoint.

9 **Green For Go** 5b From two sloping fingerholds, climb straight up to the finishing holds of *Tootal*.

10 **Deceptive Crack** 4b Harder than it looks.

11 **Biceps** 4c Climb the wall right of the crack.

12 **Easy Corner** 2b or not 2b?

13 **The Arête** 4b Climb the undercut arête.

14 **The Bulge** 5a Start at the V slot.

15 **Crack and Arête** 4b Start at the diamond slot.

16 **Thin Crack** 4a Layaway start.

17 **Suffolk** 3c The iron-stained wall.

18 **Maserati GT** 6a Start at the mini groove and climb direct. A finger ripper.

19 **Six Digit Wall** 6b To the right at a notch in the overlap.

20 **Finger Wall** 5c One foot right, direct to the slot.

21 **Fern Arête** 5a Start from the left.

22 **Step Two** 5b Climb direct from the second step of the staircase.

23 **Girdle Traverse** 5b Start at the extreme right and move left across the impending wall onto the step of the staircase (or go up *Fern Arête*). Continue round and along the wall to a rest in *Easy Corner*. Work along the diagonal crack using a foot in the scoop of *Tootal* and finish up *Yours Is No Disgrace*.

There are a couple of easier problems round on the more-public north side facing the ruins.

Other crags in the vicinity are:

SLIDING STONE CRAG   OS ref. SK531113

This spectacular outcrop with a tree growing out of it can be seen from the top of Old John. Unfortunately it is just a heap of boulders with only a little problem arête.

WARREN VIEW CRAG   OS ref. SK535118

This small crag is situated on the edge of the wooded hillside just below the water treatment plant. It faces west and is 200m east of the footpath between Swithland Wood and Bradgate Park. There are four or more good problems on the left and right walls of a V groove, plus flaky arêtes to the right. Looks a good prospect.

SWITHLAND WOOD QUARRY

OS ref. SK539122

Across the Cropston road, outside the Park, and in the middle of Swithland Wood is an old deep slate quarry with a palisade around it. The bottom is flooded and is used for sub-aqua diving (its 40m deep). The crags offer some routes above the old quarrymen's steps but none has been recorded yet. The Wood is managed as part of Bradgate Park and the warden has been known to ask you to leave. That goes for swimming too.

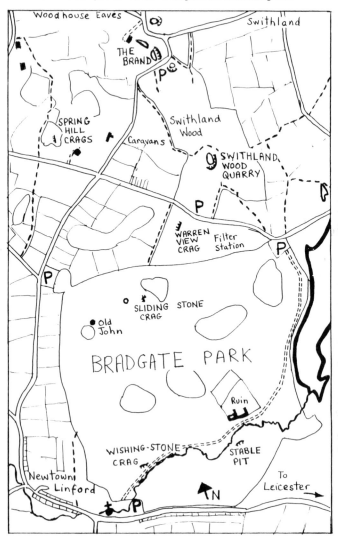

THE BRAND, SLIDING-STONE CRAG, SPRING HILL CRAG (ROECLIFFE), STABLE PIT, SWITHLAND WOOD QUARRY, WARREN VIEW CRAG and WISHING-STONE CRAG

THE BRAND

OS ref. SK537132
(Sheet 129)

SITUATION and CHARACTER

Situated in the private garden of The Brand, this crag-like quarry offers some very fine climbing on steep, often perfect, slate. The setting is idyllic especially in the sun on a summer's evening. The rock is smooth but blocky, some of the blocks having razor sharp edges. The routes are long.

APPROACH and ACCESS

Access is strictly limited to parties having permission to climb from Colonel Sir Andrew Martin, one time Lord Lieutenant of Leicestershire. You should telephone first (0509-890269) and follow the instructions given. Colonel Martin usually lets you park at the house (up a drive across a field) and has been very welcoming. Climbers are asked not to destroy the excellent relationships that exists with Sir Andrew by climbing without permission and leaving litter. It is useless to trespass because the crag is plainly visible from the house. The garden is also an area of special scientific interest because of rare lichens and other plant rarities.

HISTORY

Before the Enclosures of about 1820, stock used to be driven annually to places on the edge of Charnwood Forest to be marked with the brands of the owners. The Brand was one such place.

Slate quarrying was a growth industry in the Brand area in the 17th and 18th century. The stone, suitably dressed, was used for headstones (remember this when you climb here), guttering, water troughs, gate posts, dry stone walling and flagstones. Not much was used for roofing as the roofing slates were very thick and demanded massive roof structures. However, the slates (again ancient Precambrian rocks) last for ever, and there is a flourishing trade in second-hand Swithland slate.

The Hind family started quarrying in The Brand in 1688, leasing the land from the Earl of Stamford. They continued until 1811 when they moved to Swithland Wood. The land was purchased by the Hinds during the 18th century and sold in 1851 to the Ellis family. They continued quarrying and built the curious tower in the quarry to the north to house a pumping engine. Eventually quarrying ceased and the Ellis's landscaped the site by part filling the middle of the long thin quarry to give Trout Water and Perch Water (the climbing quarry). The Brand Estate was sold to Robert Frewen Martin in 1887 for £9,850. Robert Martin was a prominent local engineer and the managing partner of the nearby Mountsorrel granite quarry. The Martin's still own the estate.

THE CLIMBS

The crag can be split into two distinct sections. Firstly, there is Dry Walls on the right hand side (looking from across the pool) where the climbs can be approached by abseil down *Mango* onto solid ground or, by traversing from the right-hand side at the base of the crag. The Water Walls which are to the left above the pool have peg/nut belays at the base of the routes but are approached by abseil or rubber dingy!

Climbs are described from right to left as one looks across the Perch Water. The first route encountered on the **DRY WALLS** along the traverse from the right side of the crag is:

1 Fisher   18m   VS   4c
Climbers have been heard fibbing in pubs about the size of the blocks that "got away". Climb the rightward slanting fissure to the top. Loose and best left.

2 The Shallows   18m   S   4a
Climbs the next shallow groove to the top of the crag; the water beneath is shallow (and getting shallower each winter).

3 Sailaway   20m   HVS   5a   ***
Climb the "S" shaped crack by strenuous and painful hand jamming. Care is needed at the top with loose rock. An excellent route and a yardstick of its grade. Now worryingly hollow and one feels something big is going to come off sooner or later. *S. George, Bud Metcalf, Robin Prager and Ken Vickers, July 1965.*

To the left lies an obvious corner. A route has been climbed up its right wall at E1 5b but is not worth recording. Next is:

4 Mango   18m   VS   4c   **
A Leicestershire classic at its grade. The obvious line. Climb a corner by a series of superb laybacks and jams. Reputedly climbed solo by St Andrew's father before the war. *Ken Vickers and Dave Draper, Aug. 1964.*

5 Gujerati Girl 23m E5 6a **

A route that is not technically desperate but incredibly bold. From a ledge one third of the way up Mango finger traverse horizontally onto the left wall of Mango. At a thin blind flake move up (very deep breath) and climb diagonally up to a thin loose crack, and onto a ledge (good rest). Continue to a good peg (1st runner since *Mango*) and climb the blind shallow groove above to finish. *S. Allen and M. Chaney, 1988.*

Further to the left a prominent sinuous crack in the right wall of the next corner gives:

6 Modular 15m E3 6a ***

Climb the thin widening crack with good protection and very hard moves to start. It is possible to traverse in from the boulders on the left at half height and climb the crack at E1 5c *(M. Haffner, 5 Aug. 1982)*. Derek Gamble, Rick Hudson and Ken Vickers (Aid), Nov. 1965. FFA Steve Allen and J. Codling, 1983.

7 Third Time Lucky 9m HVS 5a

Climb the short corner above the jumbled blocks. Dirty but with some fine moves. *Ken Vickers and Rick Hudson, 1964.*

8 Loose Leaf 12m E1 5a

This route skirts the right side of the walls above the pool. Climb up from the top of jumbled blocks on the left of the corner to a detached pillar below a shallow groove/flake line, finish up this. *M. Hood and S. Allen, June 1988.*

The following routes are all on the **WATER WALLS** *and are described from right to left. The best method of keeping ones ropes dry is to uncoil them into a rucksack which can be clipped into the belay.*

9 Suffragette City 18m E4 5c **

The original route on the *Water Walls*, 6m left of *Loose Leaf*. This climb provides an exciting dry belay with climbing requiring a cool approach (or you'll get a cool finish). Start by abseiling down to a foot square rickety pedestal protruding from the pool and belay to the peg runner 3m above. Climb the steep wall above the belay rightwards past the tree (1st runner) to a poor peg runner, traverse right for 2m and gibber up the flake/groovelet above (crux). *Steve Allen and Ms L. Travers, 1987.*

10 Dinghy Days 15m VS 4c *

Left of *Suffragette City* is a gully; 5m further left is a flake line. Belay at the peg left of the gorse bush then climb the rightward trending flake to a small sloping ledge and go left up the blocky finish. *Ms L. Travers and Mike Hood, June 1988.*

Left again is a prominent large overhanging groove which is left unclimbed due to the rare plant life in the back. This should not be disturbed.

11 Rurp The Wild Berserk 21m E6 6b **

A route for the bold and talented, or high divers who like shallow water. This climb takes the prominent wall to the left of the large overhanging groove. Belay on the abseil rope on the right-hand side of the wall. Climb leftwards on reasonable holds (unprotected) to a rurp runner at 12m. Move diagonally right (hard) to a rurp runner, climb up and right to the top. *S. Allen, T. Reynolds, June 1988.*

12 **Fish Out of Water** 18m E2 5c ✳✳

Abseil from the only tree above the Water Walls to a peg belay 2m above the pool. Climb directly to the tree at the top of the wall passing a poor peg runner at 15m. *E. Jones and L. Travers, April 1988.*

13 **Rhythm Collision** 21m E5 6b ✳✳✳

Rhythmically between Puccini and Punk Rock. A sustained, strenuous and very technical exercise. Climb the steep groove 10m left of *Fish Out of Water* from a peg and RP belay past 4 peg runners, with some moves on the arête. On an aided attempt on this route about 1976 Ian Dring ripped out all the gear and ended in the pool. *E. Jones and J. Mitchell, June 1988.*

14 **Splash** 21m E3 5c ✳✳✳

The climb takes the discontinuous flake crack in the wall to the left of *Rhythm Collision* from a nut belay 1.5m to the left (Rocks 3 and 4) at water level. Move diagonally right and climb the flake crack (*in situ* wire). *J. Mitchell and E. Jones, June 1988.*

WATER WALLS, The Brand

CADEMAN WOOD and BROAD HILL

About OS ref. SK435170

(Sheet 129)

SITUATION and CHARACTER

The fine wooded hill to the north of the village of Whitwick contains a number of natural granite tors and bosses, some of which peep above the trees and give good views. The crags contain a number of problems, mostly easy, but some hard. It is surprisingly easy to get lost in the wood and part of the fun is actually finding the stones you are looking for (or even some others). The area is worth visiting as an area of natural beauty, even if you can't find the crags. High Sharpley is just across the road.

APPROACH and ACCESS

There are several ways into the wood.

1. For High Cademan itself there is a car park at 443168 and a short walk through the trees and over the fence leads to the summit. High Sharpley is on the other side of the road to this car park.

2. Broad Hill is best approached from the Thringstone-Poachers Corner road, or from Grimley's Rock. (See also Grace Dieu)

3. For Grimley's Rock the best approach is the public footpath up the hill across the allotments from 433168.

All the land around Cademan Wood and Broad Hill is owned by DeLisle. Historically there has been a problem with access to his land (after years of public access, High Sharpley and Gun Hill have been closed) but Cademan Wood is treated by the local people as land over which they are free to roam. And very pleasant it is too. Parts of Broad Hill are an extension of the parkland across the road in Grace Dieu Wood.

GRIMLEY'S ROCK (434169)

This is a small granite quarry to the south-west of Broad Hill and is only a couple of minutes up the hill from the road. Part of them is visible from the footpath that runs close by. This is a small slabby area which gives a route or two. A short distance further up the hill lies the quarry which has considerable potential for steep, short routes. A fine route which is difficult to start (4c) exists up an undercut slab to the right of a prominent rib at the extreme left of the quarry. There are may other prospects but the crag is deceptive and is much steeper than it looks. A warm sheltered spot that faces south.

CAR HILL ROCK (432169)

A small quarry on the opposite side of the road from Waldrams solid fuel depot on Grace Dieu Road has coal etc. stored in it. The face over the summit (facing south) should have a couple of easy routes in a pleasant open situation. This crag was called Carr's Quarry in 1911.

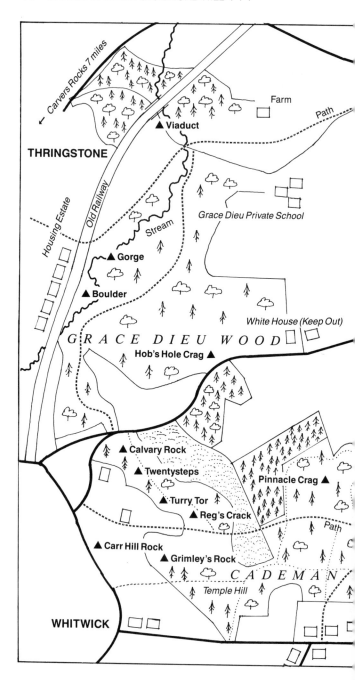

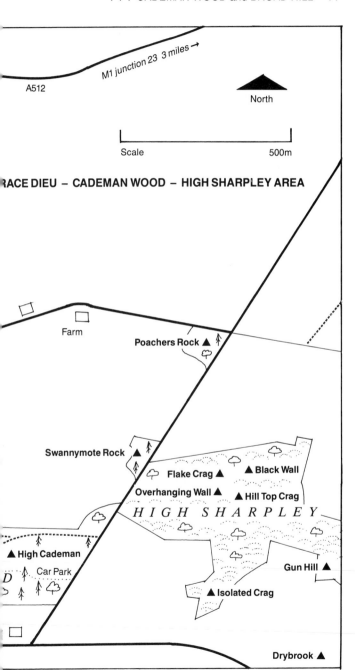

A512

M1 junction 23 3 miles →

North

Scale   500m

RACE DIEU – CADEMAN WOOD – HIGH SHARPLEY AREA

Farm

Poachers Rock ▲

Swannymote Rock ▲

Flake Crag ▲   **▲ Black Wall**

Overhanging Wall ▲   **▲ Hill Top Crag**

H I G H   S H A R P L E Y

▲ High Cademan

Car Park

D

Gun Hill ▲

▲ Isolated Crag

Drybrook ▲

BROAD HILL (from 433172 to 436170)

There are a series of rocky knolls in the strip of woodland running north-west from Broad Hill. Some can be seen from Grimley's Rock. There is a good path running from Access Point 2 towards Grimley's Rock. Most crags can be seen from this path. Calvary Rocks takes its name from the calvary erected there on Jan 1 1843, the day before a small school opened in Turry Log Cottage just below. The plinth of calvary is still there and the cross is in the Abbey just along the road. There were Fourteen Stations of the Cross leading from the calvary to the ruined chapel in the wood of Temple Hill. Presumably some of the Stations were on the tors and this may explain why the path through the woods and by the rocks is so pleasant. Is there a Twentysteps on the real Via Dolorosa?

At 435170 is **Reg's Crack**, a large boulder with a good crack.

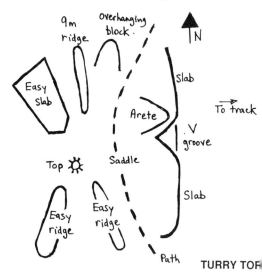

TURRY TOR

At 434171 is a crag (**Turry Tor**) with an obvious green inverted V on the east face. There is a slab and the V itself which can be finished on massive jugs. Also a fine steep arête right of the groove.

At 434172 is **Twentysteps** with a beech tree growing from the top and the remains of the steps on the way up. The tor gives a whole range of routes from slabs to the face of a blade of rock. There is a chimney and cracks. A good view from the top of the beech tree. Twentysteps is the best of the tors.

There are crags at 433172 (**Calvary Rock**) which can be best seen from the open country to the east of the wood. There are two buttresses, the most northerly sporting a 6m easy crack and a face climb. The south buttress has a more open aspect but the best rock is behind a holly tree.

The crag at 435173 (**Trilobate Plantation**) is disappointing and only the part near the road gives any climbing.

The remaining crags near the summit of Broad Hill itself are mostly piles of boulders in the trees.

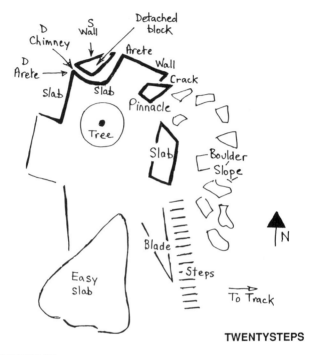

TWENTYSTEPS

CADEMAN WOOD

The easiest access is from the Whitwick-Poachers Corner road (Swannymote Road) using Access Point 1. Just to the west of the car park there is a small green, overgrown quarry with a few rocks (443168).

50m NE of 439171 there is a small crag with a pinnacle in the centre (**Pinnacle Crag**). It would be hard without the adjacent rocks. There is an arête and fine overhanging wall.

The crag marked on the map around 439171 is mostly boulders.

The trig point (442169) on the rocky summit of **High Cademan** gives a good view. There is climbing to the north around a chimney. The roof of the chockstone goes at 6a (*G. Lucas, 1987*) to a swing, a pull, and a mantleshelf. No using the feet to bridge. The left hand overhanging sharp arête is also 6a (*G. Lucas, 1988*). You may need a blowlamp to clean and dry the holds. There are other poorer prospects on **Nut Ripper Wall** (W of summit, 4m high) and **Pullover Wall** (S of summit, 3m high).

TEMPLE HILL (436168)

Provides a pleasant walk. There are many isolated boulders but none worth climbing. The old 6" map indicates a R.C. Chapel on the summit (The Temple), hence the name.

SWANNYMOTE ROCK (445172)

This little crag (probably named after the ancient Swannymote Court formerly held in the Charnwood district) is situated 100m to the east of Swannymote Road north of Cademan Wood. It is just through a wood and secure behind a wire fence. There is a small face (4m) and arête on the west side uncomfortably close to the fence. Keep your legs together if you fall off. The north face is easy but has a deep chimney. The Rock is geologically interesting because of the varied rock types there. Access probably restricted.

1 4a Left edge of arête.

2 5b Swannymote arête.

3 4c Step into middle of wall and swing up.

4 4c The wall on small finger flakes.

5 4b Thin move to big jug.

6 4b Flakes on leaning wall.

7 VD The right arête.

8 D Slab.

9 VD Chimney.

10 4c Centre of wall.

11 4b Left edge of wall.

12 D Stepped arête.

13 VD Rounded arête.

POACHERS ROCK (446175)

This little crag is situated in a wood about 100m west of Poachers Corner where Thringstone Road meets Swannymote Road. It's only 50m from the road. Access probably restricted.

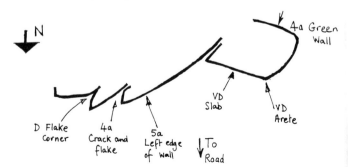

POACHERS ROCK

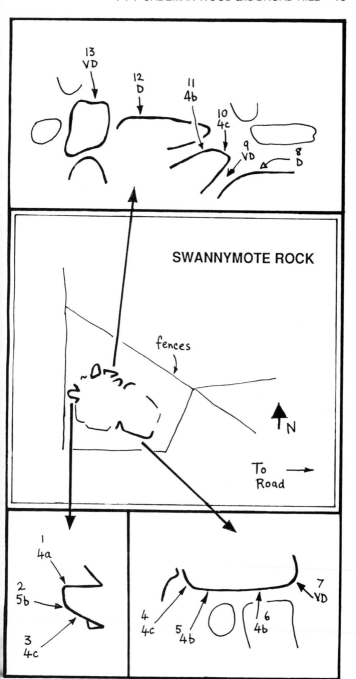

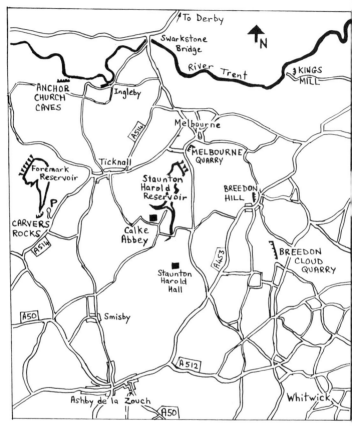

ANCHOR CHURCH CAVES, BREEDON CLOUD, BREEDON HILL, CARVERS ROCKS, KINGS MILL and MELBOURNE QUARRY

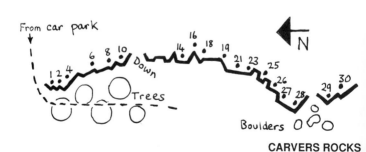

CARVERS ROCKS

CARVERS ROCKS

OS ref. SK332226
(Sheet 128)

SITUATION and CHARACTER

Carvers Rocks are part-quarried part-natural soft Millstone grit. There are trees at the top of the crag and parts are in jungly undergrowth. The quarried section has an open aspect and is pleasant in the sun. The crag faces north west and the shaded parts can be green and slippery when wet. Because of the poor quality of the rock and the excellence of some sandy landings either top-roping or soloing are the most frequent modes of ascent.

The area becomes very crowded at times – particularly sunny weekends, and the trust who manage the nature reserve are concerned about injury to other people, either by rocks falling, imitation, or by kids getting too close to the edge. The latter two can definitely be a problem so take special care (or avoid the place) at peak times and watch out for kids.

As with all soft sandstone, the crag is covered with carved initials and these give names to some of the routes. The sandstone was quarried in the 1800's for Brithy Hall and other buildings. It gave, together with the quarry at Melbourne, the best building stone in the area. The name is believed to be connected with Lawrence Carver of Ticknall (b.1701). The rocks were called Repton Rocks in 1836 and, more recently, have been termed Dawsons Rocks.

Peter Harding climbed here, just post-war, and must have done many of the routes.

APPROACH and ACCESS

The rocks are located four miles north-east of Ashby-de-la-Zouch at the southern end of the new Foremark Reservoir, just off the west side of the Swadlingcote-Ticknall road (the A514). There is a road off into a recreation area belonging to Severn Trent and overlooking the reservoir. Park here and walk back along the approach road to a sunken public path leading down west to the rocks in 200m. The car park is currently (Sept. 1992) closed as a result of pressure by the naturalists on Severn-Trent. The access route may also change but there are public footpaths which can be used to gain access.

The area belongs to Severn-Trent and a part of it is a nature reserve. There have been problems with climbing access in the past but, after involvement of the BMC, these have now been resolved.

CONSERVATION

Carvers Rocks are part of an SSSI. There is a serious erosion problem along the top of the rocks caused by general traffic, wear by ropes and the washing away of the soft rock by water flow.

In order to reduce the erosion several measures have been agreed by the BMC. More may well follow.

i)   There should be no abseiling. This will save the routes, the top of the crag, and the trees that protect the soil at the top of the crag. It is the single most important conservation measure.

ii)   When top roping from the ground use long slings on the trees so that
the karabiner hangs over the edge. This prevents the rope cutting
into the trees and also sawing into the ground. It also helps keep
abrasive sand out of your rope. If permanent bolts are placed, use
the bolts and not the trees.

THE CLIMBS

The climbs are described from left to right. The first routes are under the
trees. The first six are green and best left.

1 Jiggery   9m   S   4a
The left-hand of two cracks.

2 Pokery   9m   VS   4c
The right-hand crack, starting interestingly.

3 Carved Arête   9m   HVS   5b
Climb the arête keeping on the right-hand side.

4 Three Peg Wall   6m   E1   6a   *
Climb the peg-scarred crack in the centre of the wall. Blow-torch essential.
FFA Simon Pollard, June 1978.

5 Slimey   6m   HVS   5a
The corner, often green, just to the right of *Three Peg Wall*.

6 Pegs Climb   9m   VD
Climb the loose steep corner, finishing left. Green, vegetated and poor.

7 Flakes   9m   HVS   5a
The sandy arête to the right of *Pegs Climb*, climbed on the left-hand side.

8 Sand Pie   6m   D
The dirty groove 13m right of *Pegs Climb*.

9 Canned Arête   6m   S   4a
The arête left of *No Can Can*.

10 No Can Can   6m   VS   4c
Climb the finger-crack just right of the arête, finishing to the right.

11 Eye for a Line   8m   HVS   5b
The crack line and overhang behind the tree, awkward at the top. *I. Barnett
and M. James.*

12 The Snipe   8m   VS   4c
Start 2m right of *Eye for a Line* below an area of crumbling rock. Finish
direct.

13 Holed Wall   8m   VS   5a
Start below a small hole in the rock at 3m and continue direct.

14 Brained Crack   8m   HS   4b
Climb the crack in the middle of the wall.   Hard to finish.

15 Fingers   8m   HVS   5b
The thin crack line just to the left of *Main Gully*.

16 **Main Gully**   9m   VD
Climb the block-filled gully and up the tree roots.

17 **Crete Arête**   9m   VS   4b
Climb the left side of the arête to 5m then swing round to the right.

18 **SP 1880**   9m   S   4a
The crack just right of the arête, finishing to the left.

19 **Main Street**   9m   VD
Climb the deep crack moving left under the overlaps, to exit left of the oak tree. Or climb direct from below the tree (4b).

20 **VC 1950**   9m   E1   6a   *
The sharp arête to the left of *Zen*, from the right-hand side.

21 **Zen**   9m   E1   5c   *
Up the crack in the centre of the face, finishing direct over the two overhangs.

22 **Nil**   9m   E2   5b
Climb the slab to the right of the crack, finish direct. *P. Stidever and M. James.*

23 **Nez**   9m   E3   6a
Climb the crack just left of the gully. For a 5b variation, climb the first 4m of *Zen*, then traverse into *Nez* to finish.

24 **Slab and Arête**   9m   S   4a
The centre of the slab 4a – the left-hand arête of the slab 5b.

25 **Nutcracker**   9m   D
Climb the twin cracks, then step right to finish up the small arête.

26 **Tantalum**   9m   HS   4b
Start at "G.R. Oliver". Climb the crack and corner forming the left side of a square block.

27 **D76**   9m   E1   5c   *
Climb the left-hand edge of the block. Sustained.

28 **Gravure Arête**   9m   HVS   5b   *
Takes the bald right-hand arête starting from a boulder.

29 **Corollary**   9m   E1   5b
Boldly climb the square cut arête on the next block to the right. *S. Pollard, 8 Sept. 1978.*

30 **Lingerficker**   9m   VS   4c
Climb the cracked groove in the long wall by difficult laybacking. Has sometimes been called *Fingerlicker*.

Several scrambles are possible on the blocks and easy slabs further to the right.

CRAIG BUDDON

OS ref. SK558150
(Sheet 129)

SITUATION and CHARACTER

Craig Buddon together with the listed buildings – temples even – of the water treatment plant below the dam is a legacy of the construction of Swithland Reservoir in 1896. It is a very pleasant little quarried crag, with long climbs for Leicestershire, overlooking the reservoir and catching the full evening sun. The steam trains of the Great Central Railway make the only noise.

The rock is pink Mountsorrel granite: blocky and monolithic with runner placements non-existent. It gives balancy climbing that is serious for its grade on excellent rough rock. The rocks of the Mountsorrel intrusion only cover about 2 square miles (most of which is quarry) and are similar to igneous rocks in Scotland.

APPROACH and ACCESS

The approach is from the Quorn-Thurcaston road. Turn off the old A6 south of Quorn. Proceed for 2 miles and then turn right down Kinchley Lane. This leads towards the reservoir, dam and old water works. After a mile or so along the side of the reservoir a gated green lane leads off right from the bridge at the end of the dam and goes beside the spillway. Craig Buddon is 50m along this lane and can be reached by climbing over the gate or the wall. The crag is clearly visible from the centre of the dam.

Craig Buddon belonged to the ratepayers of Leicester, who, through the Leicester Water Board, built the dam and (now disused) water works. It now belongs to Severn Trent who permit climbing. Severn Trent have no real use for the old water works (part is used for gas training) or Craig Buddon and the area is run like a nature reserve. Severn Trent wish to monitor use of the crag and request that before visiting you telephone, the Leicester District Estates and Recreation Officer on 0509-413731. During working hours you will get information on how busy the crag might be and any access restriction. Outside working hours there is an answerphone for you to log the number of your party and the expected date and time.

The land over the wall at the top of the crag is part of Redland Aggregates Buddon Wood Quarry, the biggest granite quarry in Britain. The rock is highly prized as a roadstone because it is so slow to polish and get slippery. Despite the warning signs they seem to pay little heed to climbers walking back down from the top of the crag. The active quarry face is still some way from the top of Craig Buddon.

CONSERVATION

Even though it is an old quarry, Craig Buddon is part of a SSSI. The heather slope to the left side (north) of the crag is of special interest and although it has made a convenient way down an alternative route should be used (see below). The easiest is to go over the wall and follow it towards the reservoir. Hop back over the wall and return along the approach track. Access to the entire SSSI may be restricted during prolonged dry spells because of the fire risk and a notice will be posted to this effect.

THE CLIMBS

The crag is very compact, the most obvious feature being the black overhanging corner of Starco. On the left side of the crag there is a 5m slab which, although a little loose, gives some good traversing.

Don't belay to the small trees at the top below the wall. Their roots do not penetrate the rock and they come out surprisingly easily. Use the big ones over the wall at the top and a few long slings.

The extreme left-hand corner gives the first route (which is also a useful descent route).

1 **Dandy**   10m   D
Up a grassy ramp to the foot of the groove. Follow the groove on the left to a grass ledge and finish on the left side of the wall above. Not much use except as a way down.

2 **Cull**   10m   VD
Three feet to the right of *Dandy*. Climb up the shallow groove to the tree on good holds and finish up the wall above.

3 **Straight and Narrow**   20m   HVS   5a   *
Start below the left-hand arête. Up the steep wall to the bottom of the arête. Follow the arête via an unusual mantelshelf and a small roof to a ledge. Continue up the right edge of the short, awkward wall above. *Ken Vickers and Dave Draper, 1961.*

Two small enjoyable variations on *Straight and Narrow* exist. **Blade** ** (HVS 5a) moves right for 3m at the foot of the arête and climbs up the middle of the slab stepping out right round the arête from a ledge. **Go Slow** (VS 4b) is the obvious line and continues *Blade's* traverse right to a groove, up which the route finishes.

4 **Starco**   14m   HVS   5a   *
This strenuous climb takes the obvious black overhanging corner via some big reaches to a ledge across the lip. Continue up the arête above. Unusually for Buddon, its protectable. Harder if you're short. *Martyn Riley and Roger Withers, Nov. 1960.*

5 **Gamekeepers Refusal**   14m   E1   5b
A small amount of independent climbing. Start as for *Starco* but move up right across the overhanging wall past a peg runner. The peg further right is off line.Various claims for the first free ascent. *S. Gutteridge and P. Wells, 1978; J. Moulding, R. Conley and F. Stevenson, 1977/8.*

6 **Soft and Hard**   17m   VS   4b   *
A good route. Climb easily up the pleasant slab 3m left of *Virago* to the break (Friends). Traverse right and make hard moves up the slab to the right of the overhang.

7 **Virago**   17m   E1   5a   ***
The best route on the crag. Start at the foot of the right-hand side of the buttress. Up a clean cut groove, exiting right. Manoeuvre past the first

bulge from the right and easily up to the overhang (Friends). Mantelshelf over the overhang (interesting) and wander to the top. *Ken Vickers and Dave Draper, May 1960.*

8 **Trepidation**   17m   HVS   5b   *

To the right of *Virago* is a steep wall with a crack, the only one on the crag. Climb up to, and layback, the crack until big leaning holds on the right can be reached. A mantelshelf on the left thumb leads to the finishing holds. No bridging across the groove. *Ken Vickers and Stephen George, 1964.*

9 **Dusty Desire**   10m   HS   4b

Climb the deceptively easy–looking corner to the right of *Trepidation*. The right arête provides some relief. Once called *Dusty Diedre*.

10 **Future Times**   10m   HVS   5a   *

The right arête of *Dusty Desire* is started direct and climbed by laying away to the right. Unprotected. *Steve Gutteridge, 1979ish.*

11 **Halcyon**   12m   D

Follow the shallow groove in the slab immediately to the right of *Future Times.*

12 **Harpy**   10m   D

The crack to the right of the slab with blocks that need care. Requires cleaning with something similar to Harpic.

13 **Girdle Traverse**   30m   HVS   5a   *

Start on the right-hand side. Up *Harpy* for 6m and move left along the obvious line across *Future Times* to the break on *Virago*. Move down and left beneath *Gamekeepers Refusal* to the groove of *Starco*. Up this and traverse across the slab to finish up *Straight and Narrow*.

To the right of Harpy *there is a blocky cliff with a jungle beneath and a wall of earth on top. This is best left alone although routes have been made there.*

14 **Woden**   17m   VD

Start to the right of the main face in the centre of the wall at a rib. Up the rib move right into a groove moving left at the top through doubtful rocks with one concealed tree root for aid.

Some scope for boulder problems exists in Buddon Wood on the ridge 400m to the north-north east behind the crag. These are on some of the best rock in Leicestershire (if you can find it).

CRAIG BUDDON

1 VS   Go Slow
2 HVS Straight and Narrow
3 HVS Starco
4 E1   Gamekeepers Refusal
5 VS   Soft and Hard
6 E1   Virago
7 HS   Dusty Desire

ENDERBY QUARRY

OS ref. SP534999
(Sheet 140)

SITUATION and CHARACTER

What remains of this once extensive quarry is a poor reminder of its previous scope. One hundred foot leaning walls of blank coarse granite and fine sweeps of slab are now all buried deep under your feet. Classic routes of the early 60's such as *Euclid* and *Cacophany* have gone. All that remains is a broken area at the top of the old quarry. There were several quarries at Enderby. The climbing one is properly called Rawson's Pit or Froanes (or Frounes) Quarry. The big one to the north which is being filled in with domestic waste (note the interesting methane collecting system) is called Warren or Warren Hill Quarry. Enderby Hill Quarry (533996) and Coal Pit Lane Quarry (also called Lower Enderby Quarry) at 542992 have both been filled in. Quarrying at Enderby, which started in the 1870's, has gone full circle.

The 8m or so of rock exposure which remains after the main hole has been filled is quite extensive and might give some good bouldering. The listed climbs only occupy a small part and are heavily overgrown and need cleaning.

APPROACH and ACCESS

Enderby is just south of the M1/M69 junction 21. From here take the A46 east for 1 mile. Turn south on the old A46 (now the B4114) for one mile, turn right opposite the police station, pass under the M1 and after a mile you arrive at a cross roads in the village (church on the left). Turn right along the B582. After 500m on the brow of the hill to the right is a pub, The Plough. 250m past this on the right was an old wooden five-bar gate which led into quarry. All now overgrown. It is easier to walk through the entrance used by the lorries going to the tip in Warren Quarry and walk east to the rocks. A more discrete entrance is down the lane (it's a public footpath) by the Plough and past the entrance to a large house. As you come into the open turn left and get to the climbs.

The climbing is situated on a broken area of quarried hillside cutting into the west side of Froane's Hill for a distance of some 250m. There are short steep walls and slabs of good rock, together with more broken areas and buttresses of shattered rock.

Ownership is uncertain.

THE CLIMBS

At the left end of the face in a bay at a lower level is a blank slab finishing at half height. It is bounded on the right by an obvious cracked overhang. Look carefully as all of this is behind the trees.

1 **Drott**   10m   VS   4c
Climb the shallow corner on the left side of the slab over overlaps to finish rightwards onto a grassy bay.

2 **Hy-Mac**   8m   HVS   5a
The right arête of the slab to finish up *Dozer*.

3 Dozer   8m   VS   4c
Climb the obvious cracked overhang and slab above.

4 Scammel   8m   S
At a higher level climb the left side of the slab.

NOTES

In the centre of the face at its highest point and above broken blocks a route has been made up a pillar (no description as yet). In the right-hand corner of the main face and left of an area of steep blank rock is an obvious cracked wall, the left side of a prominent corner. This has been climbed at 4c (finish in the bushes). There are lots of possibilities here for good short problems and, with gardening, some major routes. There is a nice little bouldering slab at the far left hand end.

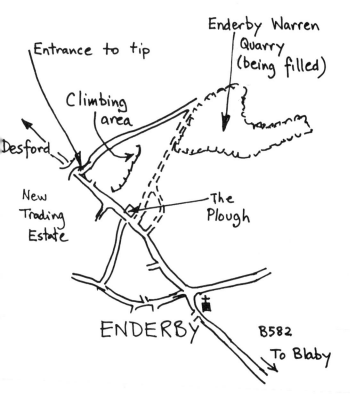

ENDERBY QUARRY

FINEDON SLABS

OS ref. SP914722
(Sheet 141)

SITUATION and CHARACTER

These are not in Leicestershire at all and are recorded here because they won't find their way into any other guidebook. The Slabs are actually in Northamptonshire. Thanks to Clive Robinson and Fraser Ball for details.

Everybody knows there is no climbable rock in Northamptonshire and they are right – the Finedon Slabs are concrete. They are really old mass concrete buttresses which have cracked and fissured to give climbable "rock". They face south and dry quickly after rain.

The Slabs are the remains of the crushing and loading plant of the old ironstone workings and are hidden away off the A6, six miles south of Kettering.

The crag consists of two sets of slabs either side of a large central roof. The slabs on the left (looking from the footpath) are known as Sun Slabs. Those to the right are known as the Swastika Slabs, with the roof being known as The Parapet, and the wall below it, the North Wall.

Routes on the slabs are delicate but the routes on The Parapet are a complete contrast, being very arm pumping indeed.

APPROACH and ACCESS

From Kettering go south on the A6 to Finedon. Just before the roundabout of the A510 turn right onto Orchard Road. Take the third turning on the right (St. Mary's Avenue). About 100m down the lane, just past a green fence, turn left along a path. The "crag" can be seen after 100 yards of footpath. There have been no access problems.

THE CLIMBS

From the bottom, facing the Slabs, on the far left of **SWASTIKA SLAB** is:

1 **Swastika**   7m   VS   4c
The centre of the left wall. Move up on small holds and gain a horizontal crack by an awkward mantleshelf. Toe traverse right and finish up the layback crack (*Orchard Crack*). *P. and S. Roberts, 1970's.*

2 **Hitler**   6m   HVS   6a
Replaces Milner Road. Climb the wall 2m right of *Swastika* on small holds to the crack at half height. Two holds on the slab above lead to the top. *F. Ball, 1984.*

3 **Orchard Crack**   5m   3c   *
The obvious layback crack.

4 **The UFO has Landed**   5m   5b
A micro-route just right of *Orchard Crack*. Needs a blinkered approach. *F. Ball, 1984.*

5 **Down Under**   5m   5b
The slab to the right. *F. Ball, 1983.*

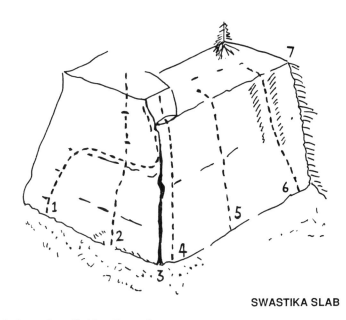

SWASTIKA SLAB

6 **Love Over Gold**   5m   6a
The slab just left of the corner with a very fierce mantleshelf half way.
Fraser Ball, 1983.

The **NORTH WALL** *boasts:*

7 **Cresta Run**   5m   4b
At the left-hand end of the wall is a corner with a thin crack. Use it, and
luck, to reach the top. Fun.

8 **Dolben Arms**   9m   VS   4c   *
Start 5m right of *Cresta Run*. Climb the wall using the three pockets. From
the top foothold reach back to the roof and escape left. Or, alternatively,
traverse right, across the slab, via the square holes (5a).

9 **Bully**   9m   5b
A boulder problem. Up *Dolben Arms* until a traverse right to *Obelisk Rise*
can be made using the foothold.

10 **Obelisk Rise**   9m   E1   5c   *
Take the slab on the left of the *two pillars* until a traverse right using the
square holes can be made to join *The Obelisk* at the cross-beam. Climb
this until a swinging traverse back left can be made using the two ring
bolts and the six holes in the beam. Finish at the corner. Very pumping.
F. Bell and G. Leonard, 1983.

11 **The Obelisk**   9m   HVS   5a

The column to the right. Climb up to the crossbar and then bridge up until a sensationally exposed swing on to the face of the column can be made (crux).   Pull up strenuously on two fingerholds and mantleshelf. Protectable. *M. Bradley and C. Robinson, 1970's.*

12 **Men at Work**   9m   E2   6a

Climb the two pillars to the right of *The Obelisk* by back and foot until an awkward position under the roof is gained. Back and foot out leftwards to place a No. 2 Friend in the lower of the three holes. Place a long (6ft) sling and return to the cross-beam. Clasp the sling and swing to a standing position. Free climb to the lip using the three holes in the roof and make an awkward move to finish. Brilliant. *F. Ball, 1983.*

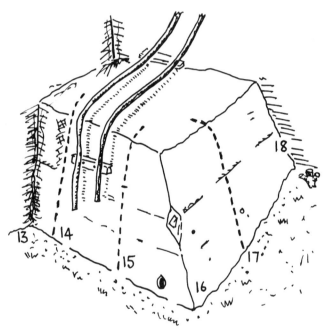

GLADSTONE WALL

13 **Mulso Arms**   5m   3c

Climb the right-hand corner of the North Wall. A natural drain.

14 **Down in the Sewer**   5m   4c

Just right of *Mulso Arms*. Wet and hideous.

15 **Gladstone Wall**   5m   4b

Climb the centre of the wall on thin holds. Using the ironwork reduces the difficulty.

16 Spectra   5m   4c
The small arête to the right. Hard to start but easier higher up.

17 Pulsar   5m   5a
Climb the centre of the next short wall on microscopic holds to the crack.
Mantleshelf to finish.

18 Easy Street   5m   1c
The easy corner to the right. A good way down.

On **SUN SLAB** *there is:*

19 Telegraph Road   9m   HVS   5c
Climb the slab right of *Easy Street*. Delicate and good. *F. Ball, 1983.*

20 Shoot the Moon   9m   HVS   6a
Climb the slab just left of the obvious crack (*Quasar*) to gain a standing
position in the horizontal crack. Take the slab above by the two enormously
spaced holds. Harder if you are under 6 foot. *F. Ball, 1984.*

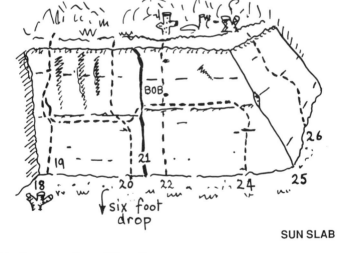

SUN SLAB

21 Quasar   9m   VD   3c
Climb the obvious wide crack on jams and laybacks. *P. and S. Roberts.
1970's.*

22 Redshift   9m   HVS   5b
Start 1m right of *Quasar*. Move up on a small knobble and make an
awkward move into the crack. Two toeholds complete this delicate route.
Was once pegged. *C. Robinson and M. Bradley, 1970's.*

23 Stairway to Heaven   13m   HVS   5c
Climb the slab right of *Redshift*. Traverse left at half height to *Quasar*. Up
this until a traverse leftwards using the numerous pockets can be made.

24 Polly 13m HVS 5c *

Climb the slab just left of the arête (*Blueshift*) to the crack at half height. Gain the crack (no using the arête) and traverse left until a line of holds up the slab is reached. *F. Ball, 1983.*

25 Blueshift 9m VS 4b *

Take the arête direct to the top. Strenuous and serious. *P. and S. Roberts, 1970's.*

26 Hammerhead 9m E1 5b

Climb the slab to the right of the arête (*Blueshift*) on the manufactured holds. No more of this, please. *F. Ball, 1984.*

27 Girdle Traverse 35m HVS 5c

Start up *Blueshift* and climb to the toe traverse of *Polly* which is followed to the corner of *East Street*. Traverse across *Pulsar* using the crack and round the arête of *Spectra*. Move across *Gladstone Wall* to *Mulso Arms* and traverse under *The Parapet* to finish up *Cresta Run*. *C. Robinson, 1978.*

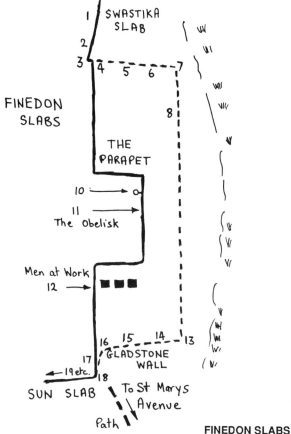

FINEDON SLABS

FOREST ROCK

OS ref. SK532142
(Sheet 129)

SITUATION and CHARACTER

Forest Rock is an old slate quarry. The crag is situated at the middle of Woodhouse Eaves, beneath the churchyard right next to (you've guessed it) the Forest Rock pub. This (the crag, that is) provides excellent climbing on good, deceptively steep rock. Most of the crag overhangs considerably and can provide good sport in wet weather. However, it rarely sees the sun and can be green in winter. The quarry originally produced a form of blue slate and was once owned by the Herrick family when it was called Great Hill. It has been called Church Quarry. The local name is currently Stone Hole. The cave was cut in pursuit of a particularly good bed of slate. The quarry was there before the church and was described in 1877 as being "long abandoned".

The slaty rock is, like all the Charwood Forest slate, very ancient – Precambrian in fact. It was once ejected from volcanoes and probably laid down in beds under water. Since then the mud has been compressed, thrust upwards and sheared (this gives the slaty cleavage). Some primitive fossils appear in a few beds.

The floor of the quarry is grassed and well tended by the Borough Council. Unfortunately about four feet of rock exposure was lost when the area was landscaped before being grassed and a couple of metres has been cut off several routes.

APPROACH and ACCESS

Woodhouse Eaves is most easily reached by turning west off the old A6 into the B591 just north of Quorn. After 2 miles turn west at the Bulls Head and follow the road through the village for half a mile. As the road starts to ascend, the Forest Rock is on your right. Only park in the pub car park if you intend to use it (the pub!).

In 1976 Charnwood Borough Council purchased the quarry under a compulsory purchase order because the place was a mess and no owner could be found. They listed the use of the land as 'Public Open Space' in the compulsory purchase order. Several years ago the old school which was adjacent to the low (useless) part of the quarry was sold and turned into houses. The top of the low crag which provides an easy way down, or a scramble up for the local kids, and has done for perhaps a hundred years, overlooks the bedrooms and backyards of these houses. Just for fun some of these young people started peeing down into the backyards and running away through the church yard. The owner wrote to the Parish Council requesting that climbing on the rocks be banned. The Parish Council referred the request to Charnwood Borough Council who decided at full council to put up a sign banning rock climbing. The Borough Council (Conservative) cynically decided to erect a sign banning climbing, even when it knew it had no authority to ban climbing. To actually ban climbing they would need a Model Bye-law from the Home Office and would be unlikely to get it as the place is public open space and not much use for anything but emptying your dog (mind your feet) and climbing on. The B.M.C. have contested the issue, and the Chief Constable is aware of it. So remember when you climb here you have a perfect legal right to

do so, irrespective of what the sign (it says "Rock Climbing is Prohibited"
the local people or a passing uninformed uniformed policeman might sa
It is one of the few crags in this guide to which you have legal acces
Please don't vandalise the sign, it only gives climbers a bad name. Do
sit on the War Memorial to eat your sandwiches, the Parish Council do
like that either. Avoid noise and bad language.

Because of damage to the small holds and nuisance to the local resider
the crag should be avoided by groups who merely want abseil practic
Use Morley or Nunckley Quarry instead.

HISTORY

Forest Rock was formerly a major centre for artificial routes. They followe
very fine crack lines in the roof of the cave, and were completed over ma
weekends, Trevor Peck's special stainless steel 'micro' pegs being grou
down to knife blades to fit the very thin cracks. Ken Vickers and Da
Draper started the ball rolling in 1959 with *Sorcerer* and *Sorceress*. Othe
were active in the early Sixties as well. The first important free rou
Definitely Not, was the bold work of Dick Wrottesley, and did not g
repeated for many years. Abseiling etc. is thought to have removed
number of the fine flake holds. The route is now much harder than in 196

A new and talented group of climbers took over the crags in the la
Seventies. The first development, was the free ascent of *Sorcerer* (*Wh
Dust Opera*) in 1978 by Simon Pollard and Steve Gutteridge. Tl
Sorcerer's Apprentice (*Wishbone Crash*) also saw a first free ascent
Steve Allen and John Codling in 1982. The action now switched
Sorceress. John Codling put the bolts in with a variety of bored (get
partners over a period of years from 1986. In 1987/8 he led the route
clipping the second bolt, failing, and lowering off. He then climbed tl
route without reloading the gear. In 1988 Torston Shutsbach, a Germa
visitor to the Leicester Polytechnic was taken to the crag by Greg Luc;
as he wanted to try his hand at the hardest route in the area. Lucas w;
under the impression that the route had been done previously by Jo
Codling. The German failed after two days effort and six falls from the
of the cave. Greg Lucas topped out instead. The first Redpoint ascent
claimed by John Codling on 24 Aug 1992.

It is difficult to see what more can be added at Forest Rock (famous la
words) but this small unique quarry is certainly an important location, ar
one of the major crags of this area.

THE CLIMBS

Routes are described from left to right.

1 Forest Wall   10m
Go straight up just to the left of the middle of the left-hand slab.

2 Definitely Not   15m   E2   5b
Start in the middle of the left hand slab. Climb the wall direct for 3m the
traverse up and rightwards on small flakes. Finally traverse above the
of the cave. A bold and serious route (No. 1 Friend required) *Di
Wrottesley, Ken Vickers 1962*.
Alternative start: 5a. From the overhanging left side of the cut awa
rock-over onto the slabby side of the arête. Go up direct to join the travers

To the right is the first weakness in the overhanging wall of the cave:

3 Senseless   10m   E3   6b
Climb straight up the short wall beneath the left end of the overlap to where it forms an inverted V. Make hard moves out from under this leftwards to a jug on the headwall. Finish direct. *1982.*

4 Sorcerer   9m   E1   5b   ***
Also called *White Dust (or Powder) Opera.* Climb the steep fingery wall left of the undercut inverted V groove, moving right to the obvious block above the groove. Continue rightwards until an excellent jamming crack leads to the wall above and the top. *Ken Vickers and Dave Draper, 1959 (aid). FFA Simon Pollard, May 1978.*

5 Saucy   11m   E3   5c   **
Climb the undercut inverted V groove and stretch over the overlap directly above for an incut hold on the left in the wall above. Follow more incuts to finish. *J. Codling, T. Johnson and S. Allen, 1982.*

6 Sorcerer's Apprentice   11m   E4   6b   *
Also called *Wishbone Crash.* An extremely gymnastic problem which climbs the downward pointing flake directly below the finger crack of *Sorcerer* up which the route finishes. *FFA S. Allen and J. Codling, 1982.*

7 Sorceress   12m   E6   6b   ***
Also called *Crypt Trip* and *Pataphysics.* Further into the gloom of the cave an obvious peg-scarred groove leads out to the lip of the overhang. Climb the groove via the crack (two bolts) to the lip. Then easily up the wall above. *Ken Vickers and Dave Draper, 1959 (Aid). John Codling 1987/8; Greg Lucas 1988; John Codling and Steve Allen 24 Aug. 1990.*

8 Top Slice   14m   A2
The only remaining aid route. From the back of the cave a series of ancient bolts and pegs lead out leftwards to some loose blocks. Either peg over these or, with a long reach, join the groove of *Sorceress* (no pegs please). A finger was badly cut on the first ascent. *D. Jump (solo), May 1976.*

There are some ivy-covered slabs opposite the main crag which might give some very easy routes (they did once).

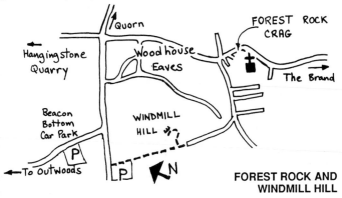

**FOREST ROCK AND
WINDMILL HILL**

FOREST ROCK

1		Forest Wall
2	E2	Definitely Not
4	E1	Sorcerer
5	E3	Saucy
6	E4	Sorcerers Apprentice
7	E6	Sorceress

GRACE DIEU VIADUCT and CRAGLETS

OS ref. SK433180

(Sheet 129)

SITUATION and CHARACTER

Grace Dieu Wood lies just to the east of Thringstone. It is old wooded parkland and some of the exotic trees are magnificent specimens. The wood is very overgrown and without people walking the old paths through the parkland the whole area would become inaccessible. Just downstream from the viaduct is a large overgrown hole in the ground. It used to be an old lime quarry but earth has slipped in and the local kids use it as a mountain bike track.

APPROACH and ACCESS

There is a map of the locality under "Cademan Wood".
There are three approaches to the climbing:

1. From the B-road from Whitwick to the A512 park either in Melrose Road, or the Rangers Supporters car park. Take the public footpath down past the Bowling Club and football pitch into Grace Dieu estate.

2. There is a hole in the wall beside the back road from Thringstone to Poacher's Corner (433172) with paths leading to the wood. This access also serves Temple Hill (see Cademan Wood).

3. There is a green gate also on the back road from Thringstone to Poacher's Corner (435174) with a path leading round the field to meet an old parkland path (runs NE-SW).

The area is part of the DeLisle estate and the old manor house is now a preparatory school.

Although the wood is private property there appears to be little restriction on access, indeed, stiles and proper holes in the walls seem to be the order of the day.
Areas to keep away from are : the ruins of old Grace Dieu Priory (435183), the big white house (437175) and the school (438179).

GRACE DIEU VIADUCT (433181)

The disused branch line (Charnwood Forest Railway, LNWR, opened 1883) that ran from Coalville to Loughborough skirts round Grace Dieu Manor estate just outside Thringstone. The railway crosses Grace Dieu Brook on a fine viaduct. To be in keeping with the parkland environment the bridge buttresses were faced in stone, gritstone in this case.

There are five buttresses, each about 10m high, and just wide enough to span with the arms. The stones protrude and provide small footholds. At the arch level one would be forced more on to the face of the buttresses. For the final 2m the buttresses disappear leaving vertical masonry.

The best approach is to use Access Point 1 to get on to the old railway track. Turn left (north) along the old railway. This is not as obvious as you might think. Follow the track for 0.5km and the viaduct is obvious. Alternatively there is access from the A512 along a public footpath past the Manor Farm. A sign prohibits access along the obvious track past the old Lodge (432182).

There aren't any climbs yet. Before you try, look down from the top. This reveals some buttresses will be easier than the others. Going north the second buttress on the right (East 2) has finishing holds. Two buttresses on the left (West 3 and 4) have tree branches which might be useful to hold you on near the top.

The best ten unclimbed routes in Leicestershire?

GRACE DIEU BOULDER (432176)

This is the remains of an old quarry which has left a 7m pyramid of rock on the edge of the wood by the brook. It can be approached from Access Point 1 to the old railway and then a short walk south. The top of the boulder can be seen from the path beside the old railway track. Alternatively use Access Point 2 and follow a range of paths, cross the stream and get on to the old railway.

There is an easy slab, steep walls, an arête and overhangs. Now getting overgrown. (See diagram).

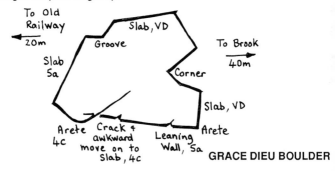

GRACE DIEU BOULDER

GRACE DIEU GORGE (423177)

The Grace Dieu Brook has cut a small gorge below the footpath of Access Point 2 just as it turns NW beside a field. There are a few very overgrown craglets that may offer a problem or two to the very determined.

HOB'S HOLE CRAG (435175)

A small green craglet boasting a huge tree. From the green gate of Access Point 3 follow a rocky ridge past boulders and the crag is visible across an old scenic path. Gives a problem or two.

WHITE HOUSE FACE (436176)

There is some rock here but it is buried so far under the rhododendrons that it's a waste of time.

GRANITETHORPE QUARRY, SAPCOTE

OS ref. SP495937

(Sheet 140)

SITUATION and CHARACTER

Granitethorpe Quarry was wrongly called Sapcote Quarry in the old guidebook. It has also been called Sopewell Quarry.

Granitethorpe Quarry is a partially water-filled hole about half a mile north-east of Sapcote village and is approached along a bridleway. The rock is diorite, related to the rock at Mountsorrel, and the whole intrusion south of Leicester has been heavily quarried leaving a string of pits. The quarry has been abandoned for some time and the vegetation is taking over in some places. However, the area at the top of the climbs is still mostly clear of vegetation and is very pleasant on a sunny day. The climbing area faces south and consists of a large slab together with an area of grooves further to the east. The water adds character to the slab but the grooves have a tree-filled ledge at the bottom. There is very little seepage and the rock dries quickly after rain. It is said that the water connects with Stoney Cove and that tipping at Granitethorpe will not be permitted for fear of polluting the Cove. The quarry was a large excavation in 1878 and contained a remarkable face of polished rock, a photograph of which appears in "The Geology of Leicestershire" by W.J. Harrison 1877).

APPROACH and ACCESS

Sapcote is halfway between Leicester and Hinckley alongside the M69 (access from the north only). From Junction 2 of the M69 take the B4069 to Sapcote. From the south take Junction 1 on to the A5. From the A5 turn left on the B4114, passing through Sharnford. Turn left on the B4069 for Sapcote.

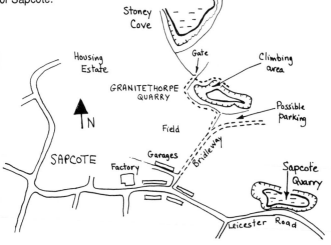

GRANITETHORPE QUARRY

Granitethorpe Quarry is best approached from Sapcote Village along
bridleway (signpost with a prominent horseshoe) which starts as
driveway leading round to some garages. It is sometimes possible to driv
the 200m or so down the bridleway and park on the rough ground by th
trees south of the quarry. Otherwise walk. Cut through into the field o
the left and get to the quarry fence. Follow this round (going west). Yo
can see the crag opposite through the wire. Keep following the fence un
a gate is reached. Go under the field fence here into the quarry and follo
the path round the north side of the quarry. The slab is easily found an
the other routes can be seen across the bay. There have been no problem
with access and the local kids fish and swim here. The best swimmin
access is on the south side down a steep earth bank just by the car parkin
spot. Ownership is unclear. There is an alternative approach going direct
across the field from the housing estate.

THE CLIMBS

First locate the **GREAT SLAB**. The first route is left of this (facing in).

1 Pretty Thing   6m   E2(?)   5c
Abseil from a tree at the top to a muddy belay. Climb the slab to a sma
overlap (crux) at half height. Continue to the top. Very poor protectior
S. Neal, 1 Dec. 1991.

2 Wish You Were Here   21m   HVS   5a
Start left of the Great Slab where it is possible to scramble down to th
water. Climb the slab following a very thin crack going slightly right. Onc
a horizontal crack is reached move left and finish as for *Unlucky Dip*.
Marchant and J. Warr, 14 July 1977.

3 The Ripper   24m   HVS(?)   5a
Abseil down the Great Slab to a small belay at the bottom left. Climb direc
to the groove in the overhanging blocks at the top. A poor jam and a lon
reach take you over. *S. Neal, 1989.*

4 The Weatherman   30m   VS   4c   *
From the belay of *The Ripper* at the bottom of the slab climb direct for 3m
Large holds lead right to a small arête. Climb this with some delicat
moves trending left at a slight easing in the angle. Top out on the left. *N
Smith and G. Massey, 11 Apr. 1974.*

5 Great White Whale   30m   VD
Start on a small rock ledge 3m above the water on the right-hand side c
the Great Slab (facing in). It is necessary to abseil down to here. Tak
a diagonal line up the slab to the block overhangs at the top and pull ove
these to finish. *M. Warburton and J. Wallis, April 1972.*

6 Unlucky Dip   60m   VS   4c
Start as for *Great White Whale* and traverse left about 7m above the wate
Go up blocks and step with difficulty on to a smooth slab. Traverse a
horizontal fault until below a fine vertical broken crack. Climb this to a
earthy ledge then move left and ascend to the top. Can be split in severa
places. *D. Ball and A. Healy, Oct. 1972.*

To the right of the Great Slab *the face cuts back to form a bay bounded by earthy slabs. It is possible to scramble down here. To the right there is a series of obvious clean slabs and grooves.*

7 Slab Route Direct   24m   S
From the bottom of the large slab by some trees, ascend to the middle of the slab on small holds which often appear to be made of mud (they come off in your hands). No protection. *G. Kelham, 21 Dec. 1974.*

To the right the slabs are cleaner. An abseil approach is easier but it is possible to traverse across.

8 Afternoon Stroll   24m   HS   4b
To the right of *Slab Route Direct* there is a small hawthorn tree at the top of a groove. Start directly below this. Climb up a small corner where two slabs meet to get to a ledge. Go slightly left up a smooth concave slab to another corner formed by an overlapping slab. Climb the corner and short wall on the right to finish by the tree. *G. Kelham, 21 Dec. 1974.*

9 Picnic   21m   VS   4c
Climb the centre of the first slab on small holds and very poor rock. No protection.

10 Harry Is A Sandbag   21m   VS   4c
Climb the steep side wall of the first groove. The crux is at 3m where the angle changes. *S. Neal, 1988.*

11 Hydro   20m   VD   *
Start beneath the first groove. The route takes the left ledge of the first clean slab direct, with an awkward mantleshelf move in the middle.

12 Hydrotactic   20m   VS   4b   *
The obvious corner groove to the right is climbed direct all the way with some obvious laybacking. *J. Gale and K.S. Vickers, May 1972.*

13 In Drag   18m   E4(?)   6b
Start 3m up on *Hydrotactic* under a small overhang. Pull over this and follow the diagonal line through small roofs (the first is the crux). No protection after the first moves. Take care with loose rock. *S. Neal, 10 July 1990.*

14 Rock 'n' Roll Suicide   16m   E2(?)   5c
Start *In Drag.* Climb the easy groove along the overhang to an overhanging block. Gain this with high footholds (or dyno). Pull over to top. Poor protection. *S. Neal, 6 April 1990.*

15 Rupert Goes Hiking   6m   S
The obvious vegetated groove (grove?). The route is now so overgrown that only the top half is climbable. A direct start is possible to the left of *Rock 'n' Roll Suicide*, very nasty. *K. Vickers and J. Gale, June 1972.*

16 Moon Age Day Dream   6m   E1(?)   5c
This is the top half of an old route called *Slab of the Evening Light (J. Gale, A. Ingram and K.S. Vickers, June 1972)* which has become badly overgrown and fallen down. Abseil down to a small belay at half height.

Climb the wall using only holds on the wall to the overlap. Peg. Using a high foothold and small fingerholds step onto the wall. Peg. Belay 15m back on a small tree. *Reclimbed, S. Neal, 7 Aug. 1991.*

Across the other side of the quarry there is a large platform. Above it, on the left, is an overhanging arête.

17 Ghengis   7m   E7(?)   6b
Climb the arête not using the crack on the right. Protection at about half height in the form of a small nut on top of a loose block. The nut also helps stop the block moving when you hang on it. On reaching the top of the arête (crux) there is no exit through the undergrowth. You should climb down or lower off from a rope hung over the top of the crag. *S. Neal, 4 Feb. 1992.*

There are other quarries (or ex-quarries) on Sapcote-Stoney Stanton axis. From north to south:

BARROW HILL QUARRY (487972) has been largely filled in but still contains some rock exposure. Once had climbs.

YENNARD'S QUARRY (Parish Pit, Charity Quarry or Rock Farm Quarry) (489970) just south is flooded and used as a local water supply.

CLINT (or **CLENT**) **HILL QUARRY** (or Stoney Bottom Pit) (490949) is flooded almost to the brim and protected by an impenetrable fence and jungle. Visible from Huncote Lane.

CARY (or **CAREY**) **HILL QUARRY** (Includes Wood's Pit and Parish Pit) (490946) was just over the wall by the cross-roads in the middle of Stoney Stanton. Now completely filled in.

STONEY COVE (or Lane's Hill Quarry, includes Top Quarry and Stoney Stanton Top Pit) (493942) is a diving centre and used for water-skiing. There is an extensive ring of cliffs but access is difficult. There is a car park in the quarry bottom, approached down the old railway. A pleasant spot on a sunny day but climbing on the rocks behind the car park would probably be dangerous, as well as a waste of time. It might be possible to hire a boat to take you round the bay to see the other cliffs. Access to some cliffs may be possible by a bay on the south side (approach as for Granitethorpe Quarry).

SAPCOTE QUARRY (497934) is just south of Granitethorpe Quarry on the north side of the road going into Sapcote from the east. It has also been called Lovett's Pit, Parish Pit, Old Quarry and Windmill Quarry. It is mostly water filled but does have a considerable amount of overgrown rock exposure. Access would be difficult although it is possible to scramble down to a fishing spot in one place.

CALVER (or Cauver, or Canver) **HILL QUARRY** (497932) has now been completely filled in.

GROBY INDUSTRIAL ESTATE

OS ref. 521076
(Sheet 140)

SITUATION and CHARACTER

Groby Industrial Estate has been built in a granite quarry that has been mostly filled in. The climbs are situated on the small amount of rock that remains above the infill. The rock is in amongst the industrial buildings. Altogether an unusual place. The routes face north and are green in the winter. This is compensated by the wooden staircase that leads from the top (its a car park) to the bottom making a very easy and unusual way back down. Past a huge steel gate there is a higher, as yet unclimbed, section of a crag. The routes listed are on the "accessible" crag. The name for the old quarry was Groby Village Quarry. It was there in 1835 and it was still working in 1910.

APPROACH and ACCESS

Groby is situated beside the A50 between Leicester and the M1. From the centre of the village take the Ratby road. After a short distance turn right following the signs to the Industrial Estate. You can see the crag straight ahead between the sheds.

Access has always been a problem as the routes rise directly off of the service road. However, it didn't seem to be anybody's function to tell you to leave. Currently (April 1992) the whole estate has been taken over by Druck and they are building a gatehouse and barrier. This may mean the end of yet another climbing area, but an access agreement might be possible because climbing has little effect on the estate.

THE CLIMBS

Starting from the left as you enter the quarry:

1 Ants Nest   5m   VD   5c
Climb up the left-hand side of the first slab on small holds.

2 The Path   5m   D
Climb the centre of the slab.

3 I Spy   5m   VD
Climb up 1m right of *The Path*.

Further to the right:

4 Buffalo Bill   5m   VD
Climb the left end of the overhang on large holds.

5 Zigger-Zagger   5m   VS   4c
Climb the centre of the overhang, also on large holds.

6 Overhaul   7m   VD
The edge of the slab 1m right of *Zigger-Zagger*.

7 Vegetation   7m   VD
The slab 1m right of *Overhaul*.

8 Groovy   7m   D
The groove 1m right of *Vegetation*.

9 Backsnapper   5m   S
Climb the left end of the wall on small holds only.

10 Torch   5m   VD
Climb the centre of the wall 1m right of *Backsnapper*.

11 Under The Steps   5m   VD
The short wall under the steps.

12 Pins and Needles   5m   VD
The obvious prominent groove under the steps.

13 The Entertainer   5m   VS   4c
Climb the centre of the slab near the steps. A long reach helps.

14 African Road   5m   VD
The right side of the slab behind a bush.

15 William   5m   S
1m right of *African Road*. On to the slab and up.

Seven metres to the right is

16 The Looser   5m   VD
Climb up the middle of the block on large holds.

17 Bramble   5m   S
1m right of *The Looser* up the side of the block.

18 Tricky Dicky   5m   S
1m right of *Bramble*, up the wall.

19 Gardener's Crack   5m   VD
The "crack" half a metre right of *Tricky Dicky*.

20 M and B Traverse   30m   VS   4c
Start 7m right of *Gardener's Crack* underneath the overhanging soil bank.
Traverse to the end of the crag at low level. Difficulty decreases to S after
the orange pegs.

Further to the right, by the orange pegs:

21 Extra Delight   9m   HS   4a
The left end of the "white" slab on small holds to a six inch footledge at
two thirds height. Transfer to *White Delight*.

22 White Delight   9m   VD
Climb the centre of the "white" slab, 5m right of the orange pegs, to the V
at the top.

*You have now reached the gate and can look through at the juicy plums
waiting to be climbed......*

HANGINGSTONE QUARRY

OS ref. SK 526151
(Sheet 129)

SITUATION and CHARACTER

This quarry provides some of the most intimidating climbing in Leicestershire. The rock is steep, smooth, sharp and unfriendly Precambrian slate, giving serious climbing of great character. It's steeper than it looks. Great in the sun but slippery when wet.

APPROACH and ACCESS

The quarry is situated 500m north west of Woodhouse Eaves, in the south east corner of the golf course. The best approach is down Brook Lane (opposite the Bulls Head – where cars are best parked for afterwards) for 400m to a track on the left between high hedges. Go up the short track, and follow the left side of the field for 200m. The quarry is on the hillside in front of you, hidden by bushes and trees. Work your way right-wards through the undergrowth and a track will be found from the golf course leading into the quarry. For a location map see "Pocketgate Quarry".

There is a deep water-filled hole in one corner, and a marl-filled ancient valley which is of geological interest. There are photographs of it in the geological books. As a quarry, the place originally belonged to the Herrick family but it is now part of Charnwood Forest Golf Club who appear to tolerate climbing.

HISTORY

The quarry has historial significance as it is one of the few remaining traditional crags in Leicestershire, many of the others having been filled in. It was first developed by Peter and Barrie Biven with Trevor Peck in 1954. This forceful trio, well know for their activities in the Peak and at Bosigran, did all the classic routes: *Holy Ghost, Christ Almighty, Crypt* and *Christ*, the latter being a local testpiece throughout the Sixties. In 1977 Leicester University climbers John Moulding, Paul Mitchell with Pete Wells and others, took the trouble to find out about the local scene and turned their attention to the smooth back wall of the quarry, producing *Weekend Warriors, Old Rock 'n' Roller* and the very hard *Sheer Heart Attack*. They also made first free ascents of the classic hard routes *Christ Almighty* and *Holy Ghost*.

THE CLIMBS

The routes are described from left to right.

1 **Left Wing**   10m   VD
The obvious broken and gorse covered buttress left of the main amphitheatre wall.

2 **Old Rock 'n' Roller**   12m   E2   5b   ***
Was once *Cloister Groove*. Climb the groove 6m right of the *Left Wing* and belay on the tree behind. A serious and poorly protected route. *P. Mitchell, S. Boothroyd and J. Moulding, 2 Nov. 1978.*

3 Weekend Warrior   12m   E3   5b

Climb the elongated peapod-shaped slot, or the wall just to its left, 3m right of the prominent corner groove of *Old Rock 'n' Roller*, until a finger crack is reached. Move delicately right and finish on two knobbles and hidden jug. *J. Moulding, F. Stevenson and R. Conley, May 1979.*

4 Sheer Heart Attack   12m   E4   6a   **

Takes the rightwards trending line of weakness up the wall to the left of the obvious crack with a tree in it. Start a few feet left of the bolt at 6m. Move up and right to the bolt, then trend back left and up, stepping back right above the bolt. Trend leftwards onto the finishing wall and boldly up. *John Moulding, F. Stevenson, R. Conley and P. Wells, Aug. 1979.*

5 Helloverhang   13m   VS   4b

Start in the right-hand corner of the amphitheatre wall. Climb the corner by ribbed blocks, which are loose at the top. John Moulding says he spent a week in Leicester Royal Infirmary with a guy who nearly died when a block fell off of this route onto him.

6 Vertex   14m   VS   4c

Climb the buttress 2m right of *Helloverhang* to the top, finishing by the small groove on the left. Poor protection.

7 Christ Almighty   16m   E2   5c   ***

Climb the next well defined groove running the height of the crag. Peg in situ at 6m. *FFA. J. Moulding, P. Mitchell and S. Boothroyd, 2 Nov. 1978.*

8 Plutonium   16m   E4   6b   **

Takes the sharp fin-like arête on its left-hand side via a thin crack to the right of *Christ Almighty*.

9 Holy Ghost   16m   E3   5c   **

Climb the rib to the right, on the right-hand side via a shallow groove which is capped by a small overhang.

10 Crypt   17m   E1   5a   **

Climbs the obvious smooth groove right of *Holy Ghost* and left of the tree at the top of the crag.

On the right is an area of a recent rock fall no doubt caused by the tree roots from the oak above. There was once a route called Sword o' Damocles (E1) here. It was a very apt name!

11 Christ   17m   E1   5b   ***

The obvious open corner to the right of the oak tree. Ascend directly to the pedestal splitting the base of the corner. Finish up the corner by some thin moves.

12 Alibi   13m   E1   5a

Climb the steep wall right of *Christ* onto a grassy bay and finish up the split wall on the left. Sorry about the gorse finish.

There was a girdle traverse across this right-hand wall starting from Alibi and finishing up Vertex. The recent rock fall makes this a dubious proposition.

HANGINGSTONE QUARRY

1	E2	Old Rock 'n' Roller
2	E3	Weekend Warrior
3	E4	Sheer Heart Attack
4	E1	Christ

HANGINGSTONE ROCKS

OS ref. SK523153
(Sheet 129)

SITUATION and CHARACTER

This series of small outcrops is situated at the centre of the Charnwood Forest Golf Club (the oldest in Leicestershire, founded 1890). Mrs Perry Herrick allowed public access to this rocky area for many years but the golf club bought its 77 acre course in 1946 (for £2,570) on the breakup of Beaumanor Estate and about 1957 stopped public access to the area. What were once spectacular outcrops are becoming very overgrown. The rocks are small, south-facing edges and consist of ancient conglomerates called, would you believe, Hanging Rocks Conglomerate.

APPROACH and ACCESS

Because of their situation in the middle of the golf course access has been restricted. However, climbers have visited the rocks late on summer evenings when the last golfers are on the tenth hole (it is a nine hole course). Climbers would cause little problem provided they approached from the clubhouse along the ridge and it is hoped that eventually an access agreement might be reached by the BMC.

The rocks can be clearly seen from Breakback Road which runs past the bottom Beacon car park towards the Outwoods. Approach from this road is difficult and it would probably be better, if climbing in Pocketgate Quarry to walk up the hill to the Rocks. If you hear a bell, watch out; the golfers ring it before driving over the blind summit.

The routes described here are reproduced from the old guide with little alteration.

MAIN OUTCROP
The climbs are described starting from the back and moving right.

1 Zimmerman Wall   4m   VS
Up the wall immediately to the left of the Shelter Stone (the large overhanging block) by awkward semi-layback. Also a hard unclimbed arête.

The Boulder is a large block to the right of the Shelter Stone and gives

2 Face Route   6m   HS
Go up the right-hand side of the face on small holds.

3 Easy Route   6m   S
Runs up the left edge. Difficult to start with a most unpleasant landing.

Coming round on to the Main Face the first climb on the left is:

4 Crossed Arms Route   7m   VD
Up the well-scratched corner moving left at the top.

5 Nil Desperandum   7m   S
Up the crack that widens into a V cleft. The normal technique is to hand traverse up the crest and then to move into the cleft. The Direct Finish is HS.

The Griffin   7m   S

About a foot to the right of *Nil Desperandum* and using none of its holds. Consists of a layback on one's jammed thumb and then *a cheval* up the small arête. Very artificial.

7 Deceptive Chimney   4m   M

The next obvious groove right.

8 Haunch of Pegasus   6m   S

An extremely strenuous arm pull over the conspicuous haunch of rock.

9 Stride and Flake   6m   VD

A route with character. Go up to the left of the flake until a good pull can be had under the flake. Stride round, and up.

10 Flake Crawl   7m   VD

An artificial route which starts direct from the bottom and goes under the flake without using it as a handhold. The antics of the leader can be highly amusing.

11 His Nut   7m   S

Go straight over the ominous bulge on the right to a delightful finish on some useful jugs.

Four Routes Wall *is to the right. With all climbs on this wall one has to be ethically strict if the grades are to be meaningful. There are cracks dividing the wall into slabs. All the footholds and handholds in the cracks are forbidden (*Route 1 *is an exception).*

MAIN OUTCROP, Hangingstone Rocks

12 **Route 1**   9m   VD
A very well worn route that still has a little character.

13 **Route 2**   9m   S
From a sloping foothold about 1m up reach for the undercut leaf of rock.
Pull outward and feel for a hold with the free hand. Finish with a delicate
problem mantleshelf.

14 **Route 3**   9m   S
Utilising very small holds go up the centre of the slab with an interesting
balance move at the top.

15 **Route 4**   9m   M
Up the groove on the right.

16 **Cracks Route**   6m   M
Up the parallel cracks

17 **Girdle Traverse**   35m   S
Start on the right. Cross Four Routes Wall and reverse the top half of
Stride and Flake. Make an exposed swing over the *Haunch of Pegasus*
Easy going until *Nil Desperandum* is reached. Almost all the way down
this until a swing can be made round a corner on to *Crossed Arms Route*
Up this to finish.

BEACON VIEW OUTCROP (523151)

About 200m to the south of the Main Outcrop is a steep little crag facing
The Beacon.

18 **The Arête**   6m   M
The prominent rib on the left-hand side.

19 **Rift Route**   7m   M
Up the slab to the left of the long groove.

20 **The Rift**   7m   S
The long groove in the centre of the face.

21 **Oak Tree Slab**   10m   S
Straight up or just right of the curious pock hold. Finish over the overhang
on good holds.

22 **The Nose**   3m   VD
From the branches of the oak go straight up on small holds.

PINNACLE CRAG (522152)

Another craglet about 100m west of Beacon View

23 **Pinnacle Route**   7m   VD
Up the face of the pinnacle. Slide down the other side and then easily to
the top.

24 **Pinnacle Wall**   6m   M
On the left up through the branches.

HIGH SHARPLEY

OS ref. SK449170
(Sheet 129)

SITUATION and CHARACTER

High Sharpley is the most surreal landscape in Leicestershire. Its name is apt – a towering sharp ridge of miniature pinnacles surrounded by a field of biscuit-like boulders. The jagged summit commands superb views, High Sharpley is just the place to be alone when everyone else is at work (or school). When you are in this lunar landscape of rock it is difficult to believe you are in mid-England.

The highest rock face is only six metres and only rarely do any of the routes exceed two or three moves. This is no outdoor gymnasium; not a place to get pumped out. The manoeuvres you make are like the place itself – unique. You climb here for the desperate mantleshelves, the frightening pinch grips and the back-breaking landings. Nothing is obvious; sometimes you start a problem from a sitting position. Sometimes you jump. High Sharpley is, like Cademan Wood, a place to play, explore and invent.

But the terrible truth is that the area may be quarried. So if you want to experience the place it will have to be sooner rather than later.

The craglets are on and around the rocky ridge which runs from High Sharpley to Gun Hill where there is an old ruin. The rock is a natural very coarse granite (actually Precambrian porphyroid) and the outcrops lie on the extension of the ridge through Cademan Wood just across the road.

APPROACH and ACCESS

The barbed wire, notices, and keepering make this the Colditz of Charnwood. The Ramblers' Association has petitioned for the right to roam. The area is owned by DeLisle and the recent restrictions on access are in contrast to other parts of the estate (Grace Dieu and Cademan Wood). Some link the recent restrictions with a plan to quarry the area.

The obvious access from Cademan Wood is heavily wired. The track from the Thringstone-Mount St. Bernard's Abbey road is also wired off.

FLAKE CRAG (446161)

This is the crag nearest Swannymote Road. It is 6m high and the climbs face north. There is a wonderful odd pinnacle with a perfect fist jamming crack up the side. From left to right:

1   VD   The face to the left of the chimney crack with blocks in it is climbed direct.

2   S   Climb on the right of the chimney crack to finish by a thin finger crack on to the right arête.

3   4b   A sinuous crack to the right of the arête. Strenuous. Use of the corner makes it VD. The landing below is nasty.

4   D   The crack in the corner.

5   VD   The right-hand edge of the outcrop direct by a high pull up.

HILL TOP CRAG (448161)

On the top facing south towards the abbey. It's 6m high.

This is the highest and most important outcrop and has an overhanging wall on which there is some strenuous and technical climbing. Be strict with yourself to get the best from the routes marked on the photo. The best landings at Sharpley.

HILL TOP CRAG, High Sharpley

RESERVOIR CRAG (448161)

On the north east of the summit facing the reservoir.

1 M Broken face left of the central crack.

2 4c The central crack with an overhang at its foot.

3 4c The two parallel cracks just left of the arête through the overhang. Bold.

4 4c Traverse on the right-hand arête (undercut base) and mantleshelf up.

BLACK WALL

Below the main summit is a distinctive short overhanging black wall.

1 5c Traverse from left to right using a sequence of bizarre wrinkles. Technical finger-tip lunges with nothing for the feet. *Greg Lucas, 1985.*
2 5b Straight up.

OVERHANGING WALL

On the north side of the hill well below the summit crags is a black overhang tucked into the hillside. About 5m high. There are no holds on the smooth wall above the overhang, only a rounded blind crack running up and over the roof. Not done yet. The right arête provides an exposed 4b mantleshelf.

ISOLATED CRAG (448168)

This superb little buttress is south of High Sharpley and near to the road junction. It has recently been partly filled with white-coloured rock and only boulder problems remain. The front face is overhanging and is split at half height by an enormous horizontal break.
1 5b A desperate mantleshelf up to a pinch grip can be had taking you straight up the middle of the face.
2 5a Traverse left to right.

GUN HILL

Low down on the other side of the hill from the ruined house is a slab-buttress. It gives a long wandering route of 4a standard.

DRYBROOK CRAG (452165)

Half a mile from High Sharpley in the direction of the abbey and near to the road. About 5m high. North west facing. This superb shaped outcrop is behind a large tree with a "PRIVATE" sign on it.

1 M The slab on the left side direct.

2 S The crack to the right of the slab by an interesting move to gain a high right foot hold using the crack and right arête only.

3 VD Crack just left of tree.

4 D The face right of the tree by the left edge.

5 D Girdle traverse at half height.

HUNCOTE QUARRY

OS ref. SP513969
(Sheet 140)

SITUATION and CHARACTER

This was the best climbing area in the Midlands, 50m faces of granite –
but with a severe access problem. Recently much has been quarried away.

Huncote Quarry is an old granite quarry (actually quartz-diorite) about 5
miles south of Leicester and close to the M1-M69 junction. The rock looks
disappointing at first sight with large broken sections and bramble cornices,
but actual contact with the many technical problems is usually a pleasant
surprise. An autumn visit could give the bonus of blackberry jam.

Unique to the Midlands, the quarry also has some long 'mountaineering'
routes. The rock requires care in places, although much of it is sound.
The finishes of some of the routes are appalling, although with care they
can be negotiated. Pegs could be useful on some of the routes, as natural
belays may not be very good. On the routes on the Rack Wall a selection
of micro-wires or R.P.s is necessary.

The quarry faces south and gets a lot of sun. Records show that it was
a deep pit in 1878 as was Croft Quarry to the south (opened 1868). It is
not known when Huncote Quarry was abandoned but Croft Quarry never
has been and has grown to a vast size. Now the active face of Croft Quarry
is beginning to eat into the old Huncote Quarry so that, instead of being
a pit, it now opens into the wilderness landscape of Croft Quarry. Just
how far Croft Quarry will go is not clear but a huge bank of over-burden
(an exciting ride on a mountain bike) has been built to screen Huncote
village from the quarry workings. Part of Huncote Quarry is so close to
the road that it is difficult to see how the face could be pushed back further.
So when some sort of access agreement can be negotiated Huncote
Quarry will be the major crag of the Midlands.

The quarry shows a conspicuous set of master-joints (which were locally
known as "slithers") together with another, more closely spaced set oblique
to these. The jointing gives a kind of bedded appearance to the rock and
gives corners and overhangs. These unusual joints, for igneous rock that
is, give the quarry the atmosphere of a natural crag.

APPROACH and ACCESS

Huncote Quarry can be reached from the M1/M69 junction (No.21), or
from Leicester, approaching the same junction and picking up the old A46
South (now the B4114) through Narborough towards Coventry. About 1
mile south of the motorway bridge turn right to Huncote. About a quarter
of a mile on the other side of the village a tiny car-park can be discovered
on the left at the entrance to a track. However, it is probably better to
continue along the road and park at the end of Thurlaston Lane (the first
turning on the right). Take the footpath back towards Huncote and various
ways in will be discovered. Alternatively go back to the layby and take a
path running round the bottom of a huge bank of earth. This leads over
a saddle and on to the quarry road from which Huncote Quarry can be
seen on the right. A slippery descent into the quarry can be made by
following the remains of an old timber tramway down a sort of ridge.
Alternatively walk further down the track and descend a giant boulder field

which has recently (May 1992) been pushed into the Quarry. Bear in mind that as the active quarry face advances into Huncote Quarry these approach details will change. (They have already — see below).

The Quarry belongs to ECC Quarries and is almost certainly covered by the Mines and Quarries Act. In the past (1970's) they have obtained court orders to prevent individuals getting access. There was even a lease to a local gun club to use the quarry for practice at weekends and in the evenings (a cunning move). But this was before the active face had broken through. Now the access position is more relaxed but it would obviously be very stupid to try to climb whilst the quarry was working. Summer evenings, Saturday afternoons, Sundays and Bank Holidays would seem to be the best times. By the time this guidebook is published the situation may well have changed (the active face is moving with remarkable speed). The routes are described here for the record and with hope that they will survive for posterity.

Note added in proof: Many routes have recently been quarried away. Posterity will weep over the destruction. Climbs that should have lasted forever have gone for a few hundred thousand tons of aggregate.

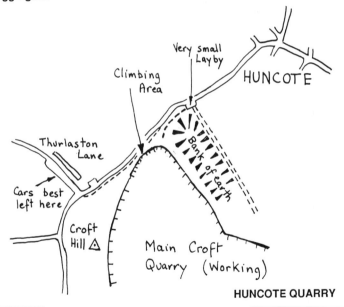

HUNCOTE QUARRY

HISTORY

Ken Vickers revived a childhood memory and 'found' the quarry in 1965. Combined with Roger Withers they kicked off with *Alleluia Road* (VS). This, together with two other routes made it into the Leicester MC 'red' guide of 1966. Competition between the LMC and the Bowline upstarts ensured that by 1972 there were some 40 free and mixed routes to go at, Vickers, D. Cooper and M. Warburton all contributing.

The LMC 'yellow' guide was published at this point and sparked off another minor explosion, *The Rack* (E1), *Stretcher* (HVS), *Little Nightmare* (E1), *The Ramp* (E2), *Sixteen Tons* (HVS), amongst others were freed by local – Mick Brady, Phil Davies and visiting raiders Wilmott, Strapcans, Harwood and the Hamper brothers, to name but a few. One activist in the 197 boom, a certain Peak climbing columnist called Browell, had the first c his recurring broken legs whilst soloing *The Ramp*. Had he broken hi wrist instead, Peak climbing history and literature might be a little different

Interest died until John Moulding freed two superb climbs – *Rack Direc* (E2) and *The Crimp* (E3) – in 1979. In 1982 Steve Allen and John Codling attacked the previously virgin Shield Wall, producing *Firing Squad* (E4) *Eton Rifles* (E4) and *Mexican Standoff* (E2), the names being inspired b the pock-marks made by rifle bullets to be found all over the wall. Rac Wall yielded two mind- and body-stretching eliminates, *Intensive Scar* and *Steel Eye Span*, both E4. Trevor Johnson got in on the act and force *Surveyor's Waltz* (E2) and Craig Dring put up *Sundive* (E2) on the fa left-hand wall to bring the quarry to maturity.

THE CLIMBS

The cliffs form two sides of the square quarry. Landmarks to look for starting from the left are : *The Shield* – the obvious imposing sheet of rock on the wall beneath the road, *The Stretcher* – a route to the right of the corner of the quarry, and *Alleluia Road* – the obvious lower crack and upper ridge of poised blocks that is passed on the descent route which follows the old timber tramway.

The climbs are listed from left to right.

At the left-hand end of the longest rock wall is a short, steep, scooped wa which can be approached from the upper tier. The next four routes star here. By now they may have been quarried away.

1 Surveyor's Waltz   21m   E2   5b, 5c.
1. 10m. Up the improbable short blank groove below the obvious rocky arête.
2. 11m. The steep juggy wall just left of a ragged crack proves perplexing near a small niche. (2 PRs).
T. Johnson.

2 Sundive   21m   E2   5a, 6a.
1. 11m. Climb the overhanging wall right of the blank groove and thence an awkward square-cut arête to blocks.
2. 10m. Precariously lay-back the leaning, rejecting overhanging faul above (2 PRs).
C. Dring and S. Yates, Aug. 1982.

3 Hanney's Hanging   30m   HS
1. 23m. Right is a large grass ramp. From beneath its left edge climb the bulging wall and crack onto grass. Climb left over easy slabs and tot, then up into a recess. Peg belays.
2. 7m. Climb the left, overhanging corner to the top.

4 **Up The Junction**   36m   HVS   5a, 4a.
1. 18m. Start below the right of three prominent overhangs. Climb up and turn the far one on the right by layback moves. From the ledge climb the rightward slanting groove to a good ledge (PB). One could abseil from here to avoid the next pitch.
2. 18m. From the left-hand end of the ledge is a leftward-slanting, blocky, groove. Follow this and exit left through vegetation.

5 **Little Nightmare**   42m   E1   5a, 5b.   **
Start at a stepped groove with three small overhangs leaning to the left directly below a big square cut arête at the left end of the lower quarry.
1. 24m. Follow the groove until it is possible to avoid the overhangs by stepping left. Step back right to a ledge below an overhang. Surmount this with considerable effort then trend leftwards to belays on a ledge under the impending red wall.
2. 18m. Mantleshelf the ledge above at its right-hand end. Step left and go up a rickety groove for a couple of metres until an awkward move rightwards gains holds on the arête proper. Continue on the right-hand side and finish leftwards. It is possible to avoid the askward moves right and to finish direct (*J. Thomas and D. Slater, Mar. 1985*). *D. Cooper, R. Andrews, I. Harley and J. Cooper, Aug. 1969*

6 **Hadji**   45m   VS(+)   4c, 4c.
1. 21m. Start underneath and left of *Little Nightmare*'s arête. Climb a finger-crack in the right-angled corner, move right and climb onto a ledge above the roof. Move up and right to beneath a short leaning wall.
2. 24m. Move right again and make an awkward swing up onto the top of the leaning wall. Climb the grassy ramp and the wall above to a brambly finish.

7 **Fusilade**   51m   VS   4c, 4b, 4c.
Start some 15m left of the *Shield Wall* below an overhanging groove which leads to a roof.
1. 9m. Climb the groove to the roof and bridge to a ledge on the left. Go up the crack to a belay.
2. 21m. Move right for a couple of metres past a large and obviously detached block to a sentry box niche. Pull over the overhang and traverse right to a corner. Up this, then move right to a peg belay above.
3. 12m Traverse left on some doubtful rock. Move up and cross the wall on the left to a break in the overhang. Climb this weakness awkwardly, to belays. Either abseil to safety or take The Eiger North Wall to finish.
4. 9m. E6, 2c. Move up the steep wall above to a niche. Escape right and then left above taking care with the movable earth slope. (A gross calumny on the Eiger).

8 **The Stroller**   45m   HVS   5a/b, –   *
Climb a series of short overhanging grooves on the left of The Shield.
1. 30m. Climb the first two grooves to reach a larger third. Climb up this to a peg runner. In the wall to the left is another peg runner. Pull up on good ledges and mantleshelf. Continue up the wall past a good edge (peg runner) to a large stance and thread belays.
2. 15m. Escape the loose blocks on the right and move back left above the stance. Ascend the nose on the left side to a tree. Reasonable exit up the short earth slope.

To the right is **THE SHIELD**, *an imposing wall rising from a grassy terrace about 10m up. It can be approached along leftward-leaning ramps starting directly below, or to the right of, the terrace.*

9 **Mexican Standoff**   30m   E2   6a   *

Below the centre of The Shield is leftward-leaning series of ledges leading up from the ground. These bring you out directly below a shothole stance, at the left end of the grassy terrace. Go straight up the groove with the shothole scar. Continue up its right-hand side (bolt) until long reaches give access to the wall on the right. Step back left into the groove. The square cut overhang is easy as is the wall above. The groove has also been climbed direct. *S. Allen and J. Codling.*

10 **Eton Rifles**   30m   E4   6b   ***

Sequence climbing at its best.
This brilliant route takes the walls below and above the slanting overlap just right. If you know the numbers, it's easy; finding out is fun. The gentle art of piton lassoing is also practiced here. Start as for *Mexican Standoff*. Step up and right until directly below a rightwards slanting overlap. Go up spaced ledges to this and make awkward moves right to clip protection pegs. Make an extensive reach from a jug just under the overlap to a poorer one. Continue in the same vein to belay at the top of the wall. *S. Allen and J. Codling.*

11 **Firing Squad**   28m   E4   5c   ***

Climb the right-hand ex-aid route free. The hard moves are near the top and the protection isn't.
The only feature in the wall's right-hand half is a slight groove at half-height and a bolt. Start as for *Mexican Standoff*. Go easily up ledges to the large ledge and move slightly right and up the wall to a very slim groove (PR). Move up and attain a precarious standing position. (BR on the right). Move up and right to a thin ledge. Awkward moves up the right-trending crack on spaced holds (PR) lead to a ledge and bolt belay. Excellent. Abseil down *Eton Rifles* to finish. (The protection bolt was placed as a humanitarian gesture after the first ascent.) *S. Allen and J. Codling.*

12 **Malaise**   45m   VS   4c, 4c.

A direct route to the top of the crag. Start 10m to the right of the wall of The Shield. There is a break in the steep walls where the long ledge cutting the cliff about 3m up comes to an end.
1, 21m. Pull over the overhang onto a ledge, then go up to a large sloping shelf on the left. Climb the groove (PR) to a stance by a thorn bush.
2. 24m. Climb the continuation of the groove. Swing left onto the arête and up to an amazing thread runner in a shot hole. Step right into the corner and go up this awkwardly to a large shelf. Go right 3m and climb the steep unstable break in the wall. Exit desperately through vegetation.

13 **Noon Groove**   42m   E1   5a, 5b.

Start at a short groove with a wedged block just left of a steep red wall.
1. 12m. Climb that groove and the twin grooves above. Step right to a ledge.
2. 30m. Follow the groove above until precarious moves up and right are made to gain a steep slab below another groove. Up this and easier ground, trending right to finish.

4 **Sixteen Tons**   42m   HVS   5a, 5b.

. 12m. Climb the groove left of the red wall as for *Noon Groove*. Step
ight across ledges to a shothole belay.
:. 33m. A short awkward groove leads to a gap between two overhanging
olocks. The awesome prow above has to be struggled over. Continue
up the groove and mixed ground above.

5. **Midnight Crack**   51m   HVS   4c, 4c, 4a.

A good climb at the lower limit of the HVS grade. Opposite the old wooden
amp are a series of overhanging cracks in the centre of the impressive
eaning wall. *Midnight Crack* takes the right-hand one. Start about 10m
eft of this at a break in the initial overhanging wall, some 12/15m right of
the obvious large smooth block. (Same as *Noon Groove*?).
I. 21m. Climb up the steep wall, by some awkward, out of balance moves,
to the large horizontal ledge. Traverse right along to it to its end and pull
over a steep wall to a sloping ledge (peg belay) beneath the main crack.
2. 12m. Climb the rib to the right of the crack for 3m. Step back left into
the crack. Climb the crack via a small ledge to another ledge and belay.
3. 15m. Climb the groove to the top of the quarry.
J. Wallis and K.S. Vickers, Aug. 1968.

6 **Daylight Groove**   39m   VS   ?, ?, ?.

The groove line right of *Midnight Crack*.
I. 15m. Climb directly up the shallow groove in the overhanging wall to
the left to the left of a pile of large unstable-looking blocks (start of *The
Ramp*) to the large ledge on the right. From the left end of the ledge pull
up onto a second grass ledge. From the right-hand end of this climb to
the belay on *Midnight Crack* below the right-hand overhanging crack.
2. 12m. Go up the groove immediately right of *Midnight Crack* to a ledge
on the right.
3. 12m. Step left and climb up the clean groove and then easier ground
to the top over the usual brambles.

7 **Xanthate**   42m   HVS   –, 4c ?.

1. 9m. Delicately ascend the balanced blocks of *The Ramp* to a ledge.
2. 24m. Fight the overhanging wall above until an awkward step left gains
another ledge below a groove. Step further left, mounting a large undercut
block with tttrepidation. Move up easier ground and climb the right arête
of the wide right-hand groove to a ledge.
3. 9m. Step left to the thin final groove/rib of *Daylight Groove*.

8 **The Ramp**   45m   HVS   –, 5b.   *

A fine route taking the obvious steep groove sloping rightwards in the
steep walls opposite the old wooden ramp.
1. 9m. Tiptoe over the obvious unstable blocks as for *Xanthate*
2. 36m. Step right and execute difficult and poorly protected moves to gain
the groove proper. Follow this with increasing ease until a traverse right
and a final steep move to gain a ledge provoke some thought. Adequate
protection is there for those who seek it.
J. Wallis and K.S. Vickers, May 1969.

19 The Crimp   45m   E3   6a, 6a.
To the right of *The Ramp* there is the largest and most overhanging wall. On the right of this there is an obvious groove line which leans against the wall with an overhang below it. Start some 15m right of the unstable blocks of *Xanthate*.
1. 30m. Follow slabby rocks until directly below the overhang. Tackle this and the groove with persistent intrigue. Move left to belay.
2. 15m. The groove above. Technical. Step up over noisy blocks to finish.
D. Cooper and R. Chuck (aid), May 1970. FFA J. Moulding, F Stevenson and R Conley, 1979.

20 Locomotor Ataxia   42m   VS   4c   *
Follow the slabby rock (*The Crimp*) until below a groove. Climb this for a move or two then step boldly right across a steep wall until an arête provides an exit to the grass ledge of *Zapata*. Finish up that route.
D. Cooper and G. Duddin, June 1970.

In January 1993, just as this book was going to press, it was discovered that all of the following routes had been quarried away. They are listed here as a testament to their discoverers.

21 Zapata   45m   HS   4b   *
A connecting of the two grooves in the corner of the quarry. Start right of *Locomotor Ataxia*. Step left and ascend the rightward-slanting groove until a blank slab interrupts progress. The moves to gain the grass ledge can prove mystifying. From the left-hand end of the grass ledge follow the groove system above, stepping right to finish.

22 Swastika   57m   S
Start just right of the *Zapata* groove. Take the easiest line until just below the overhangs. Traverse right to gain a horizontal weakness leading all the way to below a massive roof. Dodge the roof on its right and continue right to a tongue of grass. Bridge the bulge above and continue right to an easy exit up a broken groove.

23 Lupus   VS
Start a metre or so right of *Zapata* groove. Climb the crack and overhang above direct to a grassy ledge.
1. Walk right and up loose rock to belay on a ledge.
2. Climb up and right behind the belay on slabby rock.

24 Zebedee   VS
1. Climb a groove just right of *Lupus* crack and step right onto a slab. Go up this to a ledge. Belay as for *Lupus*.
2. Continue up the slab behind then follow a layback crack on the left.

25 Leprosy Wall   54m   VS
Start beneath and right of a huge overhang in the middle of the north wall of the quarry, at the foot of a short crack.
1. 24m. Climb the crack to an OH, move left onto a small foot ledge and move up to the right round some overhanging blocks. Go up to an overlap. Step right and surmount the overlap to a large ledge.
2. 30m. Move right for 5m and then climb direct to the top via slabs and a huge flake on easy ground.

26 Mayday Rib   57m   S
Start at an obvious shallow groove right of *Leprosy Wall*, just right of an earth mound.
1. 27m. Climb the groove and move right under an undercut rib. Move up and left round the rib. Move onto the rib and then up to a grass ledge beneath a overhang.
2. 30m. Move slightly left and then back above the overhang. Finish straight up trending slightly left.

27 **Tummy Rumble Groove**   48m   HS   *

Start beneath an arête 15m right of the huge overhang and 3m right of *Mayday Rib*.
1. 12m. Climb the arête and trend right to a steep groove.
2. 12m. Go up the groove to a ledge and move rightwards into another one. Climb this to a ledge.
3. 24m. Climb the wall, avoiding a projecting block until it is possible to traverse rightwards across a slab and into a corner. Take this to the top.
A. Edmonds and R. Singleton, May 1968.

28 **Cod Liver Oil**   42m   VS   *

Start as for *Tummy Rumble Groove*.
1. 24m. Climb the arête and cross the grass ledge on the right to a groove. Go up the slabby right wall to a ledge. Climb the groove to a good ledge. (Junction with *Tummy Rumble Groove*).
2. 18m. Climb the wall above to a ledge and then go up the slab to a corner. Nice pitch.

RACK WALL *is the large clean area of walls and slabs with overhangs at half height at the north-east corner of the quarry. It offers some of the finest climbing in Leicestershire and the routes have very pleasant finishes. (Surprise, surprise).*

The first route follows a corner with blocks on the left and Rack Wall *on the right.*

29 **Bella Donna**   45m   VS   *

Mantleshelf up the wall just right of a blocky corner. Continue up a groove to a flat ledge. Step left round a bulge to a groove. Follow this to the top.

30 **Ballistics**   30m   HVS   5a

Abseil down *Bella Donna* to a bolt belay. Traverse right above the roofs on *Rack Direct*, then up the first groove.

31 **The Ripper**   45m   E2   6b

The left arête of the obvious groove of *The Stretcher*. Climb up to the cave beneath the roofs (just below the stretch of *The Stretcher*). Pull over the roofs on the left and directly up the wall to a bolt. Using the arête move up the wall to make a precarious reach for small holds. Proceed directly. *D.J. Slater, Mar. 1986.*

32 **The Stretcher**   45m   HVS   5b   **

The elegant and pleasant groove above the left-hand end of the overhangs. Start up a small groove 6m right of the blocky corner. Step left and continue up past small overhangs to a large ledge (possible stance). From its right-hand end make interesting moves up then stretch back left into the base of the groove. Up this finishing rightwards on the wall above.

33 **The Rack**   45m   HVS   5a   *

Takes the centre of the overhangs and then traverses right to finish up grooves on the right of the headwall.
Follow the wall 6m right of the shallow groove to the base of a rickety flake. Follow this and go over blocks above to a narrow ledge under the overhangs. Traverse right under these past pegs (crux) to the base of a groove. Step back left and finish up this.

34 **Heat Treatment**   45m   E2   5b/c   ***

Also known as *Rack Direct*. Superb climbing straight through the centre of the overhangs. A brilliant solution to the roofs. Follow *The Rack* up the flake, through the blocks to the pegs (or start at a loose weathered scoop and go straight up a very shallow groove, *D. Slater and J. Thomas, Apt 1985*). Bridge through the overhangs above the pegs. Unusual moves enable holds to be reached above a second smaller overhang. The slab above proves problematical. *FFA J. Moulding, P Wells, R. Conley and F Stevenson, 1979.*

35 Intensive Scare   45m   E4   6a

The counter-diagonal to *The Rack* is a modern eliminate with some ha
and necky climbing although not in the same places.
Start at the right-hand end of the buttress. Climb up leftwards on ledge
until a step right can be made to a knifeblade in a slab. Make worryir
moves up and left to start then back right to better holds. Trend leftware
to blocks. Go over these to a small ledge on *The Rack*. Climb the overhan
a few feet left, where a crack splits it. Trend diagonally leftwards on
steep slab to the base of a shallow scoop/groove. Make very thin move
in this scoop to easier ground. (Potential monster from here). Finis
above. Excellent route. *S. Allen and J. Codling.*

36 Steeleye Span   45m   E4   6b/c

An alternative to the upper section of *Intensive Scare* giving the harde
climbing in Leicestershire. Telescopic reaches on minute holds add 1
the excitement of being 40m out and above the overhangs.
Climb as for *The Rack* to the overhangs. Move up to the crack that goe
through the overhang on the left (*Intensive Scare*). Trend rightwards un
balancing on small footholds. Stretch up on imagination until a small ho
high on the left is reached. Pull up on this (long reach) to a foothold ar
respite. *S. Allen and J. Codling.*

To the right of RACK WALL *there is a larger and more broken grassy fac
with a prominent ridge of tottering blocks on the right (*Alleluia Road*). Th
is* ALLELUIA WALL.

37 Necrotic   48m   S

Start 15m left of *Alleluia Road* at an obvious easy groove starting left.
1. 24m. Up the groove for a few feet, then move right over a cleft bloc
to a grass ledge and belay.
2. 15m. Move up and left through the roofs then up a short groove with
tree at its head to a grass ledge.
3. 9m. From the right of the ledge move up rightwards to the top.

38 Deception   51m   VS

Take the second groove line at the top.
1. 24m. Start as for *Necrotic* to the grass ledge and belay.
2. 27m. Climb the groove on the left until it peters out beneath a wal
Swing right to another groove and follow this to the top, moving left c
right at the final roof.

39 The Un-original Route   51m   VS

Take the third groove left. This is the central one, with a bush in it abou
9m from the top.
1. 24m. As for *Necrotic* to the grass ledge and belay.
2. 27m. Climb the groove above and right past two small bushes. The
loose final section is turned using the groove immediately right.

40 Bee-bop-alula   45m   HVS   5a, 5a.

1. 24m. Start up the overhanging recess 9m left of the *Alleluia Road* crack
Continue up broken ground to under a roof crack. Traverse right beneath
this to gain more broken ground and a flat stance beneath the grooves.
2. 21m. Layback and bridge the groove above. After an awkwar
mantleshelf traverse 6m right for an easier finish.

41 Chicken Run   45m   HVS   5a, 4c.

1. 24m. As for *Be-bop-alula* to the flat stance.
2. 21m. Climb the wall right of the right-hand groove. Continue direct.
J. Harwood, May 1969.

42 Puckoon   48m   VS

Start 4m left of *Alleluia Road* at a thin crack.
1. 12m. Climb the wall to a tree belay.
2. 15m. Climb to a ledge and bush then up the short, smooth wall usin
a faint crack-line to an obvious cleft block protruding from the ledge.
3. 21m. The slabby wall above is divided by a broad overlap in the shape
of inverted V. Climb up to near the apex from the left, then move directl
up until it eases. Traverse right to exit, or more difficultly, climb trending
to the right, then make directly for the top.
M. Warburton, R. Withers and K.S. Vickers, April 1968.

43 **Alleluia Road**   51m   VS   4a, 4c, –   *

A landmark climb. Find this one and it will help locate the others. From the descent in the quarry an obvious shattered arête appears on the right, with a steep wall split by a crack at the bottom.

1. 12m. 5a. Climb the crack to a stance on a prominent block on the right. Abseil off a tree or continue with:-

2. 9m. Climb the front of the arête through large blocks.

3. 30m. Climb the ridge to the top.

S. Vickers and R. Withers, 1965.

Direct start - *Hail Mary*, 15m, E2, 5c, *A. Blowers, May 1992.*

44 **Green Meat Grooves**   48m   S   *

Start 6m right of *Alleluia Road* at a series of obvious grooves running up a rib.

1. 21m. Climb easily to a large grass ledge and then up the obvious groove to a small ledge.

2. 27m. Go up the groove moving left at the top to a short V corner. Go up this to grass. Easy scrambling to the top.

M. Warburton and R. Hudson, Feb. 1967.

45 **Girdle Traverse**   310m   HVS

A tremendous excursion traversing the entire crag from left to right. Start on the terrace on the left:

1. 30m. Traverse from the terrace across to belay on *Little Nightmare*.

2. 15m. Move right and up. Step down and round to an overhanging niche and make an awkward move right to belay by a large bush.

3. 12m. Continue round to below a conspicuous crack. Move down, and round the nose. Traverse the short bulging wall and belay on *Fusillade*.

4. 45m. Move down 3m and step off the lowest ledge on to the wall. Peg. Move across and up to a runner on *Stroller*. Step down and traverse the grass terrace to a steep diagonal ramp. Climb the ramp and traverse right to belay on *Malaise*. A serious pitch.

5. 12m. Descend *Malaise* for a few feet then climb round to belay through a shot hole on a large comfortable ledge.

6. 18m. Move right and climb the short wall by a shallow groove on the right to a constricted niche. Move up and climb the short grooves above to an exposed belay below a very clean groove. A superb pitch.

7. 9m Move right round the arête to a peg above an overhanging wall. Use this to place a good channel peg and pull across to a system of ledges. Traverse these to belay on the edge of *The Ramp*.

8. 24m. Abseil down *The Ramp* then traverse round to a belay below the large overhanging wall.

9. 18m. Move across to the wall. Move up (as on *Locomotor Ataxia*) to reach a small ledge. Hand traverse this and then up to a good handhold. Go up to belay on *Zapata*.

10. 48m. Move up and along the line of weakness to a large ledge. Descend to a small stance. This pitch traverses across above the large overhangs about 15m from the top of the quarry.

11. 27m. Move up and along good ledges to the vegetation. Pass this precariously. On to belay on *The Stretcher*. A poor pitch.

12. 18m. Traverse across beneath the overhangs. Cross the overhangs as for *Rack Direct* and continue round past an old railway line to a good stance and thread belay.

13. 30m. Step right and climb up the short wall to a ledge. Go along this to a hawthorn bush and then follow the arête of *Alleluia Road* to the top.

Beneath the buttress which the wooden ramp leans against there are a few short routes. This small buttress forms a promontory. The routes described are on the small steep wall facing Croft Hill trig-point.

46 **Dringle**   9m   VS   4c   *

Climb the wall just right of the left arête.

47 **Dangleberry**   9m   VS   4c   *

Climb the obvious thin crack in the middle of the wall, stepping off the large ledge to start. Good.

48 Raspberry   9m   E1   5b
The small problem corner to the right of *Dangleberry* and the descen
route. *D. Slater, Mar. 1985.*

CROFT CRAGS (SP512959, Sheet 140)

*Nearby in Croft Village are a series of ancient small quarries (512959),
beside the Soar. They face north. They are a very recent discovery bu
look promising.*

*The crags are in the centre of the village over the river opposite the
Heathcote Arms. The rock is good pink granite (quartz-diorite). The area
is in two parts. The first part is wet underfoot in winter, although this does
not effect the climbing. The top of this section of crags is close to a graden
boundary so make no nuisance; don't make noise, belay, or traverse off
along the top. There are many trees and easy descents. The second
area is beyond the stone wall in the field. No routes recorded yet.*

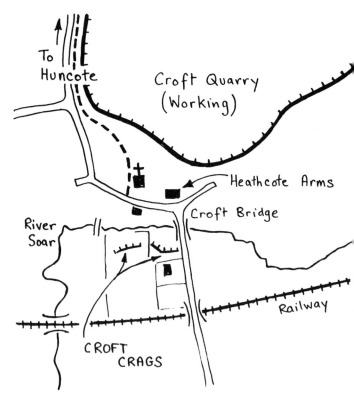

CROFT CRAGS

LOUGHBOROUGH UNIVERSITY CLIMBING WALL

OS ref. SK512186

(Sheet 129)

SITUATION and CHARACTER

The climbing wall is outdoors and unlit and so it is not much use in the winter. However, it faces south-west and can be very pleasant on a summer's evening. The wall is about 15m long and 5m high. The holds are a mixture of bricks, recesses and rocks all fixed in a vertical brick wall. Very good for the fingers but no cracks. There are no anchorages at the top so once you get up you have to get down again. There are a variety of routes but the repeated traverse is probably most popular. Passing on this is difficult and so the wall is crowded with one or two climbers. The pea gravel at the bottom means that you can jump off from quite high and land comfortably.

APPROACH and ACCESS

From junction 23 on the M1 take the A512 to Loughborough. Take the first turning marked "University" off to the right. The road is currently (June, 1992) being dualled and so these instructions may be outdated. The turning into the University is a dual carriageway. Go to the T junction and turn right under a building which bridges over the road. There is a car park on the right and the wall can be seen just down the hill.

Although on private ground the University has an open campus and so access is not currently a problem.

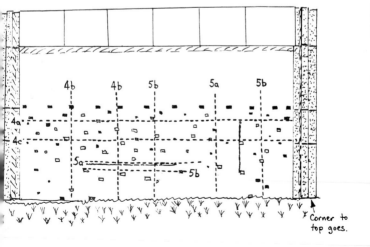

LOUGHBOROUGH UNIVERSITY CLIMBING WALL

MARKFIELD QUARRY

OS ref. SK48610

(Sheet 12∫

SITUATION and CHARACTER

Markfield Quarry was active in 1830 and large scale extraction began
1852. By 1863, Ellis and Everard who operated it employed 90 me
Quarrying ended about the turn of the century. Some of the granite w
used for curbstones, setts and building but a lot went for roadstone. Th
rock is Markfieldite and the quarry is the type-locality for this igneo
intrusion. The date is uncertain but it is certainly later than the ancie
Precambrian rocks of Charnwood. Called Hill Hole locally.

The quarry is on top of a hill – and is in two tiers. The lower tier (pit)
filled with water to a depth of about 5m. Since the quarry fills only w
rainfall and loses water by evaporation, the water level can vary over
range: a factor of importance on several of the traversing lines. The wat
in the quarry is uncontaminated by organisms from outside and this h
kept Markfield's crayfish free of an imported disease. Apparently America
crayfish, imported for harvesting, have contaminated British rivers with
disease which kills the English crayfish. Markfield is one of the few area
that has escaped and contains the genuine healthy English crayfish. Th
crayfish are a protected species which might save the quarry from bei
filled in, a fate not unknown in Leicestershire. They are the second highe
crayfish in England, the highest being in Malham Tarn. The quarry is goo
for an evening swim and scuba diving (don't use gear wet from elsewhe
– remember the crayfish) and provides excellent and extensive climbin
of all grades. The top is often loose and belays infrequent. Soloing
frequently attractive although a life-jacket is desirable in some place
Many sections catch the full evening sun. The noise from the motorwa
is a nuisance in places.

The quarry is owned by Tarmac Roadstone who have displayed variou
warnings about entering the area. However it is regularly used b
motorcyclists, divers, young kids, young lovers, dog exercisers an
climbers and there have been virtually no problems of access to date.
should really be public open space. During a recent water shortag
Tarmac pumped out a large volume of water to serve their existin
workings at Cliffe Hill. The level has never returned to normal, sligh
altering the nature of one or two of the routes. Planning permission wa
granted in 1980 for the quarry to be filled in. The permission has no
lapsed. It certainly appears an ideal site for waste disposal of some kin
No doubt it will happen one day which is a pity since the quarry doe
contain a number of worthwhile routes, *Baptism* must rank as
"Leicestershire Classic".

At first sight the quarry is disappointing. Although it is huge there are larg
areas of unclimbable rock and extensive vegetation. In particular, larg
parts of the full-height section have been almost irretrievably lost to th
thick gorse. The rock is variable: some is hard, other soft, gritty and loos
there have been one or two major rockfalls over the years. Neverthele
Markfield is an important and popular venue for Leicestershire climbing

APPROACH and ACCESS

The quarry is one mile south-east of the M1-A50 junction (Number 22). It can be seen on the top of the hill on the right when driving north on the M1. Take the A50 towards Leicester and turn off to Markfield. Turn off before the village and follow the "Industrial Estate" sign. The quarry is obvious, on the left. There is a convenient lay-by (rubbish dump) opposite a large hole in the fence (there are several). In spite of all the large rusting signs prohibiting access there have been no problems. Indeed the quarry is used by all-and-sundry as a recreation area – so be prepared. The quarry is situated on the hill to the west of Markfield village.   Access is possible by walking up a public footpath from near the church or better through one of the aforementioned holes in the fence.

Recently (April 1992) a new fence has started to circle the hill and it may be that Tarmac are taking a renewed interest in using the place. By June most of the fence was gone, a victim of local vandalism. Damage said to be £3,500. However, the posts may be useful as belays.

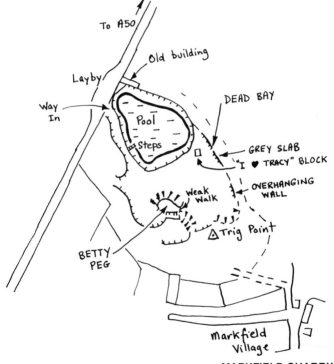

MARKFIELD QUARRY

THE CLIMBS

The quarry is a crater in the top of the hill. There is an obvious extensive platform at the level of the hole in the fence above which is the upper tier. Below is the water-filled tier with routes starting at the waters edge. On the north side this platform has been quarried away and the routes run the full height from the water to the top. In the south east corner of the upper tier there is a peninsular of rock running into the quarry (the Betty Peg) and this has a fine rocky south face.

The routes are described for the **UPPER TIER** first, starting from the north corner where the Upper Tier starts as a separate entity. This is across the water from the flight of concrete steps (to a disused pumphouse) and near a block which was once painted "I ♥ TRACY". Tracy is obviously now unloved as the sign is part obliterated, but still visible.

On the left along a narrowing path there are several possible lines. The most obvious is:

1 **Big Crack**   9m   not done
Climb up to the obvious crack about 7m left of the rockfall scar at the left end of the undercut slab. Make your way over the grass ledges to the top. Will be possible when the gorse bush occupying the crack is removed.

2 **Concrete Banana**   9m   HVS   5b
Start 5m left of the rockfall scar. Climb slightly rightwards over overhangs to the left hand end of an obvious ledge at half height and below the notch of *Wall Climb*. Now, step boldly up round to the left onto a hanging slab (crux) and finish direct. *C. Hunter, 1973.*

3 **Wall Climb**   9m   S   4a
Start just left of the rockfall scar. Follow a leftward trending crack line to a sandy and tricky finish through the obvious notch and on to a wall of blocks in the mud – or climb back down!

4 **Trend Right**   9m   not done
Follow *Wall Climb* to the obvious ledge at half height and the trend rightwards up the slab just above the rockfall scar.

DEAD BAY AREA

The next 6m of rock have suffered a number of rock falls and are in a dangerous condition.

Just to the right of the rockfall is an excellent 6a boulder problem, trending leftwards up to the centre of a clean wall.

Just right again a sandy slanting groove provides the next route.

Looseflake Crack   7m   VS   5a
2m left of the obvious corner of *Dead Bay*. Ascend the leftward trending line to a tricky finish. *H. Pell.*

Speed King   8m   E2   5b
An obvious challenge. A landmark you can't miss. Climb the S-shaped crack just left of *Dead Bay*. Strenuous, brutal and loose - but protectable. *J. Moulding, F. Stevenson and S. Boothroyd, 1979.*

Dead Bay   8m   VS   4b
Climb the steep right-angled corner by bridging and long reaches.

Dead Arête   6m   S   4a
Climb the stepped arête to the right.

There is now an easy way down. Just right is a small pedestal, **THE CIOCH**.

Cioch Wall   8m   S   4a
Climb the face of The Cioch to a grassy ledge. There is a rusty old bolt in the wall. Trend leftwards up the wall to finish.

0   Cracked Wall   8m   S
Start 2m right of the bottom of The Cioch. Climb the crack and the top wall above.

There is now a loose section but 7m to the right of Cracked Wall *an obvious crack goes diagonally left.*

1   Titch and Kwacker   12m   VS   4c
Climb up to the crack. Ascend it, and step over the large roof on the left to finish up the awkward corner. *Tony Crofts and Brian McGaw, October 1978.*

There is now a loose section but round to the right is a large slab, **GREY SLAB**. *There are stake belays at the top.*

2   Left Arête   11m   VD
Up the cracked groove of the left arête of the slab.

3   Left Edge   11m   VD
About 2m right of *Left Arête*. Climb up over the bulge and finish more easily.

4   Black Slab   11m   VD
About 4m right from *Left Arête*. Climb up the middle of the black slab, moving a little leftwards past a dovetailed shot-hole (if you can find it).

5   Grey Slab   11m   S
Climb straight up the slab about 2m left of the hairline crack in the centre.

6   Gorse Slab   11m   VD
Climb the slab following the continuous hairline crack, a little right of centre.

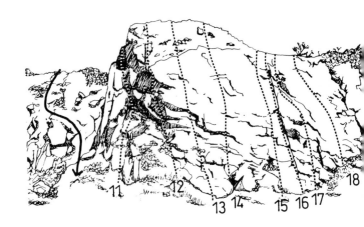

GREY SLAB

17 **Just Right** 11m VD
Straight up 2m right of the hairline crack of *Gorse Slab*.

18 **Babbies Bottom** 11m S
*
The smooth slab just right of *Just Right*. Best at the top.

About 40m to the right a prominent nose sticks out of the top of the blocks

19 **Nose Arête** 6m S
Step up from the left over the big roof and climb the arête beneath the
nose.

*About 12m further right, behind some trees, and holding some hard
problems is the clean short* **OVERHANGING WALL**.

6b The left wall, trending right.
6b The centre groove direct.
5c Start to the right of the centre groove and reach high and left for a
square hold at the top of the groove. Pull up over into the grass.
5b A rising rightward traverse to a large right handhold by the grass. Get
the top and pull over.

*The face now deteriorates. There is a vegetated buttress beneath the
trig. point (which may give a long route or two to those with a strong
stomach), and a wooded bay topped by the rocky ridge connecting the*
Betty Peg *to the trig point.*

*The next climbs are on the right hand face of this bay on the north-east
face of the* **BETTY PEG** *There is an obvious sloping weakness starting
from the right of the buttress. It looks rubbish, but gives some good
climbing.*

20 **Whist** 15m HS 4b
Fight your way along the bottom under the wall for 10m. Straight up, over
the little roofs and exit left.

1 Contract Bridge 17m S 4a

Start below the leftward sloping little niche which is about half way up the face. Climb straight up, into the niche, and step up and left past a useful little gorse bush. Easily up left to finish. *J. Tomkins and S. Keogh, 19 Jan. 1974.*

2 Weak Walk Direct 20m VS 4c

Start about 3m left of the right toe of the buttress. Straight up a little groove and the bulge above to the slab of *Weak Walk*. Left up this to the large block ledge below the top. Pull strenuously up the wall on the right on good holds to the top. *J. Tomkins and S. Keogh, 19 Jan. 1974.*

3 Weak Walk 20m S 4a ***

The star route. Start at the right hand toe of the buttress by a short wall. Climb up and leftwards on to a leftwards-inclined undercut slab. Up leftwards to the large ledge beneath the top overhangs. Make an exposed swing up right on good holds to easy ground, and the top. Much better than it looks. *K.S. Vickers and G.W. Boulton, 1973.*

There is now a steep, muddy, easy way down and a steep north-facing grass slope with a mossy slab at the bottom.

The west tip of the Betty Peg *is scarred by several easy ways down. The next routes are round on the South Face of* Betty Peg *on* **BETTY'S SLAB**. *They catch the full afternoon and evening sun and provide routes of all standards. Often, the hardest moves are at the bottom making soloing a reasonable option. Exceptionally for Markfield, there are belays at the top. Routes are described from left to right.*

4 Elderberry Crack 5m D

Start at the left of the slab by a little triangular cave behind the elder tree. Bridge up over the cave and up the slab to finish.

5 Elderberry Corner 8m VD

Start behind the tree beneath the corner. Up a little slab. Then pull boldly up the corner crack. Continue the line to finish.

6 Sugar Daddy 9m HVS 5a

From *Elderberry Corner* reach up the arête for a jug and make a bold swing up right, round on to the slab. Continue more easily. It is possible to make two more moves up *Elderberry Corner* and step right on to the jug making the climb Severe.

7 Gollywogs Cake Walk 25m VD *

Start at the bottom left of the slab by the elderberry tree and make a rising rightward traverse across the face using the obvious break for hands or feet as required. Finish just round the right edge of the face. Can be split into two pitches. A long route for hereabouts.

28 Crown 10m S *

Start as for *Gollywogs Cake Walk* but continue straight up the slab on good holds.

29 Hard Shoulder 10m HS 4b *

Start 4m right of the tree at a broken weakness. Up over the bulge and then more easily to the top. *R. Hazelwood, 1963.*

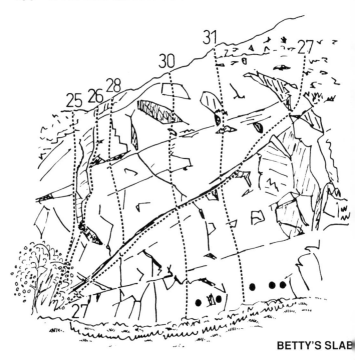

BETTY'S SLAB

30   Clearway   10m   S   **

There are a row of six holes at the bottom of the slab. Paleomagnetism studies by Leicester University? Start at the leftmost hole. Straight up to the ledge at half height. On up the top wall past a big jug in the fault line.

31   Go Home   12m   D

Start between the middle pair of holes. Straight up to the big ledge and on to the top by the easiest line.

32   Fast Home   15m   M

Start at the bottom right hand corner of the slab and take the obvious weakness up to the left.

At the back of the bay holding Betty's Slab *there is a rock step leading to the shorter second tier,* **UPPER BETTY'S SLAB**. *This contains some superb rock problems, often close to the ground. There are also some continuous longer routes but boldness is needed on the rock of the uppermost section. Protection is minimal.*

33   Bramble Edge   7m   VD

Start by the big blocks at the left. Up the polished groove stepping right at the top.

34   Thorn   7m   S   4c   *

Start in the obvious scoop near the ground 1m right of the left arête. Up the scoop. Pull out on excellent fingerholds and then climb more easily to the top.

35 **Fork**   7m   VS   5a
Up the slab 2m right of *Thorn* using an undercut flake.

36 **Slow Home**   7m   S
Climb the obvious polished weakness 4m right of the left edge of the slab to just right of the birch tree at the top. This has a useful root for a finishing hold. Mind the tree doesn't come out.

37 **Teaspoon**   7m   S   4a
Straight up the slab about 1.5m right of *Slow Home*. Carefully over the blocks at the top or step left.

38 **Nick's Way**   7m   HS   4b   *
Start 3m right of *Slow Home* and follow a rising leftward line to finish by the birch tree. If you're lucky the right hold appears at exactly the right time.

39 **Kate**   9m   VS   4c   **
Named after the bush. Start 4m right of *Slow Home* at a huge foothold. Straight up the slab making a hard move (crux). Step right at the gorse bush (if she'll let you) and up to a ledge below the final slab. Move up in a fine position to get the jug. And so to the top.

About 3m right of Kate *is an obvious crack line leading up to a mini slab below a roof.*

40 **Celeste**   9m   HVS   5a
Up the slab just left of the crack line and finish up *Kate* (with some cleaning of bushes separate finishes could be made).

41 **Quariantics**   13m   HVS   5a
Up the crack, traverse 3m right across the mini slab below the overhang and finish boldly up the loose top wall. *D.N. Draper and K.S. Vickers, June 1963.*

42 **Phobos**   13m   HVS   5a
No description, but you can guess where it goes.

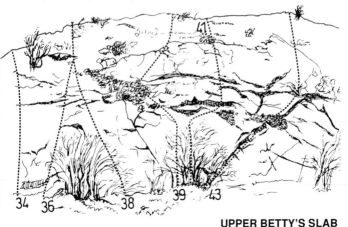

UPPER BETTY'S SLAB

43 **Cake Walk** 25m D
Start at the foot of *Quariantics* and follow the rightward rising traverse line with an awkward move by the gorse bush on good holds. Finish up the slab to the left.

Just right of the Cake Walk *is a desperate little slab which gives a couple of problems getting off the ground. Then there is:*

44 **No Overtaking** 12m D
At the extreme right of the slab make your way pleasantly up the cliff.

45 **The Ramp** 25m VS 4b
Start at the bottom right hand corner of the slab and traverse upward and leftwards along the fault line. Pass under the overhang with difficulty but good holds. Finish up *Kate* (!) or traverse through the gorse bushes which need cutting off.

46 **Girdle Traverse** 30m VD 5a
It is possible to traverse the whole length of *Upper Betty's Slab* just a few feet off the ground. Better than a climbing wall.

Most of the Upper Tier on the way back to the entrance hole in the fence is grass and gorse. There is a small wall of worthwhile rock just off the track by the top of the concrete steps which gives some problems.

The **LOWER TIER** *is partly filled with water which makes access a problem, but adds spice to the water-level traverses. The routes are described starting from the bay below the "I ♥ TRACY" block. The bay catches the evening sun and makes a good swimming spot. It can be reached by an easy scramble down. The bay is across from the concrete steps that lead down to the disused pump house. The bay is the starting point of* Baptism, *one of the best routes in the quarry.*

A real hazard about soloing the traverse lines above the water is the possibility of falling off, banging your head and being unconscious in the water. It is best to have someone around who can pull you out.

47 **Baptism** 50m VS 5b at high level ***
                                  4c for the low-level variant.
                                  E3 for non-swimmers

From the bay walk around the grass bank. Up this and traverse the undercut slab to its left-hand end. Move down across a steep wall to a hard move into a dirty corner lapped by overhangs. There is an old peg here.
Traverse down across a wall to the left and continue the traverse at water level enjoying the transformation from sound rock to loose vegetated choss. *D.T. Holyoak and P.J. Howard, Oct. 1970.*
4c low-level variant: if the water is low (and you have long legs) it is possible to make a giant stride and pull across underneath the initial overhang and continue to complete the first section.
On the second section swing down the borehole on the right and traverse left centimeters above the water. Rejoin the main traverse. Impossible at high water.

48 Font   24m   VS   5a

Follow *Baptism* for 7m and then up the overhanging V chimney. Up the groove above with a step up and right to join the top of *Hedgehog*. Follow this unpleasantly to finish. *D.T. and D.M. Holyoak, Sept. 1970.*

49 Holey Water   40m   VS   A1

Start as for *Baptism*. Follow *Baptism* for 16m past the hard move down to peg belays beneath overhangs left of the chimney taken by *Font*. This point can also be reached by swimming, by reversing pitch 2 of *Baptism* at VS, or by abseiling through a break in the overhangs to the left and swinging in to the rock near water level.
11m. Climb the shallow bulging chimney slightly left of the stance, then an easier angled crack tending right to small stance and peg belays. Four pegs used (removed) for direct aid; two might be enough if they were already in place.
12m. Move up to right from stance to join *Hedgehog* and follow this leftwards to finish through steep gorse. *D.T. Holyoak and P. Moate, 14 Mar. 1974.*

50 Hedgehog   20m   S

Start at the same point as *Baptism*. Walk across the grass bank. Go up the slab to the right to gain the corner above. Follow this for 5m then traverse left and up the gorse covered slab towards a small hawthorn tree. Not worth the pain.

The bay immediately below the "I ♥ TRACY" block has an overhanging wall from the left of which grows a tree. The next two routes lie on either side of this wall.

51 Prickly Pair   6m   VD

Start just to the left of the tree and climb the green crack onto the obvious block. Finish direct.

52 Prefabricated Pomegranite   7m   S

Climb the obvious leaning corner to the right of the overhanging wall. The un-named arête to the right is also of interest. *C. Hunter and T. Brice, 25 Feb. 1973.*

The next few routes can be reached either by abseil or by traversing above the water from the bay below the "I ♥ TRACY" block, towards the pumphouse steps.

53 Crab Crawl   15m   S   **

Traverse right (facing in) from the boulder beach for about 15m until a downwards sloping ramp is reached. There is an obvious crack line running up to the right. Follow the crack line and finish up a steep little corner behind a hawthorn bush.

54 Tap Dance   20m   VD

Start about 3m right of *Crab Crawl* (just left of *Without Friction*) below an obvious slanting ramp and traverse up it in a fine position. Either finish up *Crab Crawl* or make a step left round a band of poor rock to gain an easy rock ridge. Follow it pleasantly to the top. There is an easy way down just left of this finish.

55 **The Drain**   15m   VD   *

Start just right of *Tap Dance* at the foot of the corner that is the drain of the little pool. Follow the corner until the delightful slab on the right provides cleaner climbing. Better than it looks.

56 **Without Friction**   15m   VD

Start at the foot of *The Drain*. Traverse right up on to the slab, then follow the line of weakness past a tiny earth ledge, keeping left at the top. Loads of friction.

57 **Bic**   10m   VS   4c/5a

Traverse the short obvious leaning wall midway between *Without Friction* and *Chequered Slab*. It's obvious from the pumphouse steps. *Alan Little, 27 July 1981.*

58 **Chequered Slab**   12m   VS   4c   **

Opposite the wall of *Baptism* an obvious quartz-marked slab rises straight out of the water. Unfortunately approach is by abseil and there is no stance at the bottom. Other routes possible here.

58

CHEQUERED SLAB

There are a couple of mossy slabs to the right of Chequered Slab *and to the left of the pumphouse steps. There are some equally unattractive lines up to the right of the steps. The next routes are 50m to the right (facing rock), just below the way in and the hole in the fence.*

Immediately below the road is obvious blank wall with a crumbling red brick wall above. **POOL WALL** *once rose out of the water, but refuse tipped from the road and the recent drop in water level have removed the need for abseil approaches. All routes are now approached via a steep ramp to the left of the wall (facing in).*

59 **Dropsy**   13m   VS   4c

A poor route taking the crack system on the left hand side of the wall. Start directly below the crack. Up the wall to the crack. Follow this to a loose earthy finish.

60 **Plain Sailing**   14m   E2   5c   **

Has been called *Chariots of Fire (J. Codling and S. Allen)*, and takes the centre of the wall past an obvious protection bolt. (The bolt replaces a poor peg placed lower and to the right). Start at the left-hand end of the obvious rising traverse line. Follow the break until directly below the bolt. Move up leftwards, clip the bolt (if you feel the need) then make difficult moves up right and past it. Continue delicately but more easily to the top. *P Stidever (solo), Apr. 1983.*

61 **Arrows of Desire**   18m   E3   6a   *

Traverse the break until about 2m from its end. Thin moves lead straight up to a handy ledge and the top. *S. Allen and J. Codling.*

62 **Puppy Love**   16m   VS   4c

Also known as *Burning Bow* but unfortunately *Puppy Love* came first. Called *Gas Oven Traverse* when using 2 pegs by *M. Hoffe and A. Cuddy* on 24 May 1972. Follow the obvious rising traverse line to its end where loose rock and grass provide a tricky finish. *Steve Davies and Mick Nadal, March 1980.*

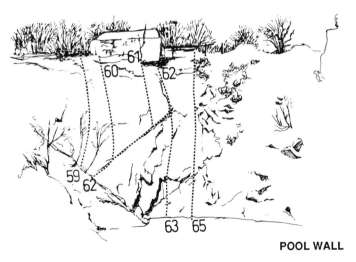

POOL WALL

63 **Scratchins**   13m   HVS   5b

Start 4m left of the obvious corner of *Trundlers Reward*. The climb has a serious feel as the rock is poor. The climbing however is good and sustained. Ascend the crack and overhang (crux). Continue, trending slightly rightwards to finish as for *Puppy Love*. *Trevor Gunner and Colin Fowler, Sept. 1978.*

64 **Crocodile Sandwich**   13m no grade available

The blank wall between *Scratchins* and *Trundlers Reward*. Awaits a first ascent?

65 Trundlers Reward   13m   HS   4b
Climbs the prominent corner crack to the right of the wall. A difficult start enables the crack to be reached and followed to another loose earthy finish. *D.T. and D.M. Holyoak, Sept. 1970.*

66 Bigwigs Bundle   13m   E1   5a
The unprotected arête to the right of *Trundlers Reward* is climbed direct. A jungle bash is avoided by traversing into the corner at the top.

Continuing rightwards there is no climbing worthy of record until the clean **WHITE SLAB** *rises from the water to the full height of the quarry. The right side (facing in) of the slab can be reached by a path running down from the top. The slabs face south and gorse is beginning to take over. The gorse, however, is more solid than some of the blocks at the top.*

67 The Worm   25m   VS   4b (machete for aid)
Traverse left across the slab towards a small hawthorn tree. Move up and then continue left below overhangs on vegetated ground to a possible belay. Continue directly above to reach the large hawthorn by the least vegetated route. Very unworthwhile.

68 Pink Slab   25m   VS   4b
Straight up the bulge in the centre of the White Slab moving slightly right to an obvious scoop leading through the overlap. Move left and up to the top. Now make your way up an unpleasant earth slope to the safety of the gorse bushes.

69 White Slab   40m   S   4a   *
Traverse the White Slab from its bottom left corner via the obvious line near its top edge to a vague and vegetated rib. Move up to a vegetated ledge and get to the top. Makes a good finish to *Baptism. D.T. Holyoak and Miss D.M. Sager, Sept. 1969.*

70 Soft Route   25m   VS   4b
Start 15m right of the White Slab and at the end of the descent path where a prow of rock juts out above a clean slab. Climb the slab and continue awkwardly up the obvious corner to the right of the prow onto a large vegetated ledge. Move up left and finish via a vegetated slab.

71 Decrepitation   25m   HVS   4c
Start at the groove line 8m further right. Climb this on frighteningly loose blocks to awkwardly and boldly exit left to finish as for *Soft Route.*

72 Trepidation   23m   VS   4c
Start up the leaning rib on the right of the buttress leading up to the overhang. Surmount this awkwardly to a slab and traverse left to finish as for *Soft Route.*

Half way down the path leading to White Slab *there is a small bay,* **MASTER'S WALL***. This has some superb unclimbed clean south-facing steep rock.*

Nearby are the **ALTAR STONES** *(484109) with a spectacular fractured cockscomb ridge which, sadly, gives no climbing. They are public open space and, although noisy, are good for a picnic.*

MINOR OUTCROPS and BOULDERS

KINGS MILL   OS ref. SK418275
In Quarry Wood.   Isolated quarried sandstone outcrops of 6-7m in woodland. Well vegetated and no known routes.

MELBOURNE QUARRY   OS ref. SK383249
A sandstone quarry on the south side of the village, approached down a track by the allotments. The quarry has been part-filled but about 10m of clean rock remain. Several good crack lines. A new house is being built (Sept 1992) at the end of the track but it is not clear whether the quarry will become the garden (like the sandstone quarry at the end of the bridge in Stanton by Bridge). This quarry was once full of beehives and the bees and climbing didn't mix. The bees have gone now and only empty hives remain. No known routes.

BREEDON HILL   OS ref. SK406233
A prominent local landmark. The hill has been quarried back to near the church. The limestone is no longer quarried but the site is used as a store and works and is probably covered by the Mines and Quarries Act and so access will be restricted. No known routes.

BREEDON CLOUD   OS ref. SK413213
This is the working limestone quarry associated with Breedon Hill. Contains some slabs which have been climbed on. Because this is a working quarry access will be restricted.

RATCHET HILL   Around OS ref. SK448164
At the south side of open woodland are a series of small outcrops and boulders (try 449165, 448164 and 446163). A pleasant spot best approached from the path that now runs along the south side of the wood. The quarry is now much bigger than shown on the current OS map.

HIGH TOR   Around OS ref. SK454158
In a wood overlooking Mount St. Bernard's Abbey. At the south end of the wood near the quarry is a fine pinnacled arête. The face of this is split by three cracks providing short, but good, problems. Round to the left is a steep face with a thin crack and swing away to the right (VS) (try 454158). Many more short, steep walls and boulders (try 453157 and 454157). High Tor is a must for jungle bashers. Best approached from the path along the south side of the wood but choose your spot.

WARREN HILLS   Around OS ref. 460150
Once called High Towers, the Warren Hills one of the few open moorland areas left in Charnwood Forest. The rocky escarpments facing SW look impressive but do not amount to much. At 461148 is an old quarry which gives a long scramble but is overgrown. At 463153 is a large rock with a slab on the N side. The fragments of different rock (or "bombs" as they are sometimes called) embedded in the bulk rock make excellent holds. This rock is well off the public footpath so trespassing here can incur the wrath of the naturalists (see Oaks Pinnacle).

IVES HEAD   OS ref. SK478170
Short problems in a very pleasant situation.

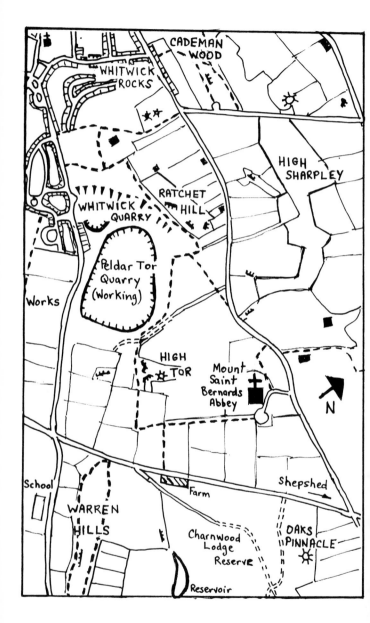

CADEMAN WOOD, HIGH SHARPLEY, HIGH TOR, OAKS
PINNACLE, RATCHET HILL, WARREN HILLS, WHITWICK QUARRY
and WHITWICK ROCKS

BILLA BARRA
OS ref. SK466114

A small old slate quarry near the top of Billa Barra hill has a small face which gives bouldering. There is a pool nearby, at the top of the crag! A beautiful spot with views marred by the new Stanton quarry below. Owned by Tarmac, as is much land hereabouts. Best approached from the east up a fence line in the field beside the house.

GROBY A50 QUARRY
OS ref. SK 519078

There is a small miserable noisy quarry with poor rock just beside the A50.

BENSCLIFFE WOOD
OS ref. SK513126

Situated on top of the hill in the wood on the left-hand side of the road leading from Old John to Shepshed. There are a number of short flake and slab climbs. The location (and sometimes, picture) is in all the geology books because it is the "type locality" for the Benscliffe Agglomerate, a variety of Precambrian rock.

BUCK HILLS
OS ref. SK511158

On the left of the road from Woodhouse Eaves to Nanpantan a concession footpath goes beside Charnwood Hall, a County boarding school. The path leads to a N-S ridge. Along the ridge to the S are a couple of small crags and a pool (511158). The concession path leads N (the other branch goes to the top of the Beacon) and runs along a delightful ridge above a valley. There is a pinnacle of 8m (only Mod) just below the path (507164) on land belonging to the Nanpantan Hall Estate. If continued E the concession path comes out on to the road again.

SPRING HILL CRAG (ROECLIFFE)
OS ref. SK527127

Spring Hill Crag is in a wood 100m east of the footpath which runs north from the B5330 across the golf course. The rock face west and give three or more good problems (4b-5a) on short undercut buttresses in a fine spot.

WINDMILL HILL
OS ref. SK526127

On public land adjoining the open space of Broombrigg's Farm just north of the old windmill. Mostly easy boulder problems but one very hard (6a) arête. The best boulder arête in Leicestershire? *G. Lucas, 1987.*

NANPANTAN HILL
OS ref. SK501170

In a wood on the south side of the road, plainly visible.

TWYFORD VIADUCT
OS ref. SK742093

About 10 miles NE of Leicester. There are very good traverses and bouldering as well as aid routes on the arches.

TRENT BRIDGE
OS ref. SK583384

In Nottingham on the south-east side of the river by Nottingham Forest football club there are many problems (from 5a upwards) on the bridge stonework. 6c traverses in the outermost tunnel.

UNIVERSITY WALL
OS ref. SK 541380

A stonework wall in the grounds of Nottingham University gives pleasant traversing at about 5b/c on two tiers (3m and 2m) beside the lake. There is a natural crag nearby and an indoor wall at the University Sports Centre.

FOREST WALL
OS ref. 568413

In Nottingham. This built sandstone wall is approx. 10m high and 100m long. Goes anywhere at 5a. Gives a very long tedious traverse.

MOAT CLIMBING WALL

OS ref. SK596042
(Sheet 140)

SITUATION and CHARACTER

The Moat Climbing Wall in Leicester is located inside Moat Community College. This is situated 500m NE of the London Road railway station, on the corner of Maidstone Road and Sparkenhoe Street.

The Wall is a corridor shape with climbs on both sides and ends. Its surfaces are of breeze-block with rock holds and concrete cracks for most of the wall and brick with chipped holds for the two bolted walls. The wall is 6.8m high to the walkway at the top and offers about 85 square meters of climbing surface. On the walkway there are top-rope bars that cover all of the breeze-block surfaces. There is a small changing area from which the walkway can be reached by a fixed ladder.

Groups (see later) are advised to limit their numbers to 20 since the floor area is quite small and the ventilation is poor.

APPROACH and ACCESS

When approaching by car head for the city centre until the inner ring road is reached. Then follow the ring road clockwise if approaching from the N (or anti-clockwise if approaching from the S) until the Swain Street traffic lights are reached. These are opposite the Leicester Mercury building with its digital clock and thermometer. Turn left if going clockwise (right for anti-clockwise route) at these traffic lights and go over the Swain Street bridge (the railway) on to Sparkenhoe Street. Take the first left on to Maidstone Road and first left again for the College car park. The wall is located in a separate locked room inside the College, next to the sports hall.

Because of regular block bookings the Wall is rarely available in the evenings from Monday to Thursday .

BOOKING

The wall is operated on a booking system based on 90 minute sessions. From Monday to Friday the wall is open from 9.00 am to 9.00 pm during school terms and from 9.00 am to 4.30 pm out of school terms. The wall may be available for booking on Saturdays and Sundays from 10.00 am to 4.00 pm if there are sufficient bookings to cover costs. To book the hall, users should phone 0533-625705 or write, Moat Community College Maidstone Road, Leicester, LE2 0TU.

The wall is only hired to groups (min. 2 people) who Affiliate to the College (current fee £20.00 per group). The cost of booking the wall for a 90 minute session during the 1991-92 school year was £4.00 (School or Youth groups) and £5.50 (Adult groups). Groups that want to make regular bookings should contact the College for details.

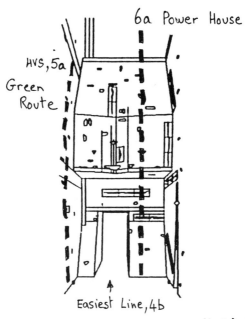

6a Power House

HVS, 5a

Green Route

Easiest Line, 4b

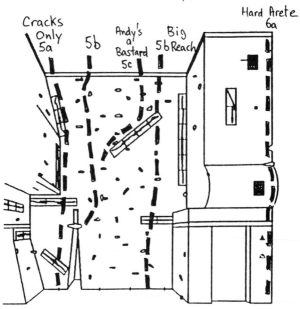

Cracks Only 5a

5b

Andy's a Bastard 5c

Big Reach 5b

Hard Arete 6a

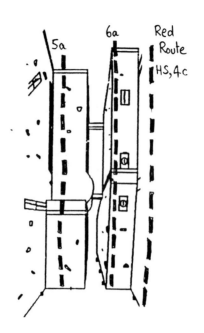

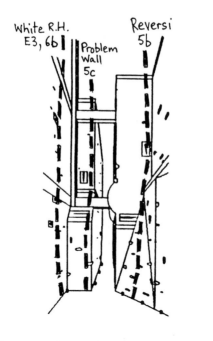

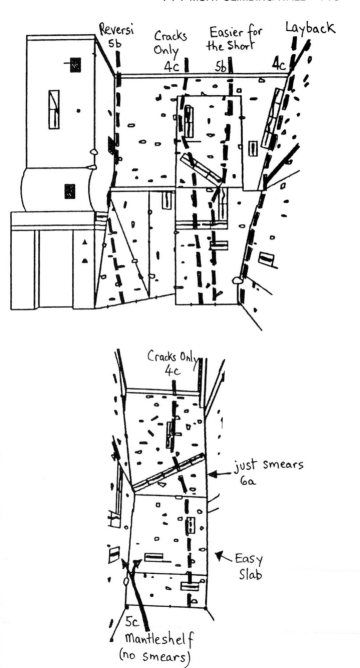

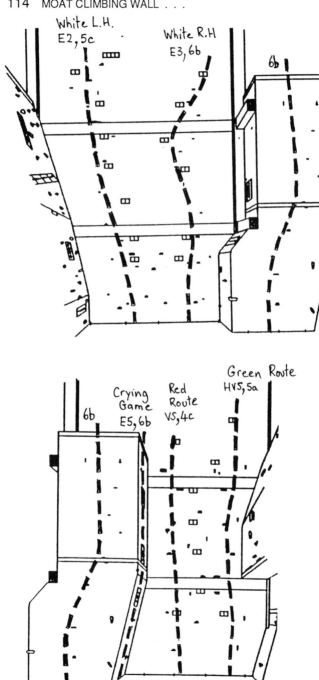

MORLEY QUARRY

OS ref. SK476179
(Sheet 129)

SITUATION and CHARACTER

Morley Quarry is situated half a mile south of Shepshed and offers new routes in the "Cornwall Shale Cliffs" vein. Although the rock is not shale you may wish that it was. Most of the quarry faces north but it is large enough to have an open aspect and the face to the east is quite sunny.

At first sight the quarry is impressive. A closer inspection reveals that the entire south wall (it faces north) is topped by marl deposits which are about 3m thick. So even if you get to the top of the rock, there is a long way up vertical dried clay to the top. No doubt the stones embedded in the mud would help . . . .

The only routes recorded so far are on the small entrance walls. The entire main quarry is unclimbed – but not unclimbable. There are some good lines, but cleaning from the top is essential.

The quarry is quite old. The small quarry with the pool (see later) was there in 1835.

APPROACH and ACCESS

From junction 23 on the M1, take the A512 towards Shepshed. After one mile (the second traffic lights) turn left towards Oaks in Charnwood. 200m up the hill on the left is Morley Lane which leads along, bearing right just before the cricket club, to the quarry. Limited parking by the gate. Take note of the warning signs.

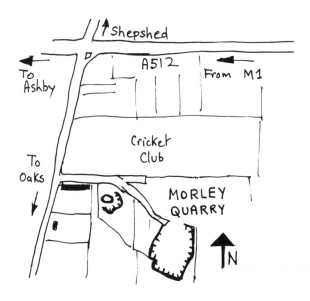

MORLEY QUARRY

The quarry belongs to Charnwood Borough Council who acquired it for climbing. A small fortune has been spent clearing the foot and putting up the fences. Unfortunately without clearing the overburden from the top and scabbing off the loose rock, the place is useless, if not murderous.

The Council have deliberated on what to do. A shooting range and caravan site have both been proposed. Even filling it in (hooray). However, all has come to nothing because local residents want it left alone. So it's still there beckoning.

THE CLIMBS

On the right of the entrance lies a steep wall of relatively sound rock forming a crenellated arête. The first three routes are here and are on the low part of the wall on the entrance side of the earth bank. The tree of *Derek's Dilemma* is the best landmark.

1 New Rose   7m   HVS   5a   *
Climb the wall left of the overlaps starting at the horizontal drill scar. Move up to the horizontal break (peg runner). Make a difficult move right to finish on good jugs.

2 Teresa's Crack   9m   VS   4c
Climb the rightward slanting crack 6m left of *New Rose*.

3 Derek's Dilemma   7m   HVS   4c
2m left of *Teresa's Crack* is an obvious tree with a bent trunk. Step off the tree and climb the wall trending left to obvious flake holds.

The next routes lie on the opposite (left) side of the quarry entrance on a graffiti covered buttress.

4 Builder's Arête   15m   VD
Climb the slab and up the arête to a loose finish. Tree and fence belay.

5 Latent Wall   15m   HS   4b
Climb the slab and then move left along the break to climb the wall above direct. Traverse right and finish up the arête.

200m to the west is a tiny crag above a small pool which gives some interesting problems. Some think it's a better place than the main quarry.

NOTES

Potential for new routes abounds for those looking for steep loose climbs. It is just possible that if enough people were stupid enough to climb here then the place might become cleaned up enough to become safe. But look around and you will see that large pieces of what looks like safe rock in the main quarry has recently fallen down and shattered into small fragments. Just like the Blackbrook Reservoir Crag. But then, the rock is very similar. Again Precambrian, but age has not improved the quality.

It has been suggested that one solution to the dilemma of Morley Quarry would be to place bolts at the top of the clean climbable rock (this is the wall at the south of the quarry) either by abseil or by long ladder. The routes would terminate at the bolts and the wall of mud would never need climbing.

MOUNTSORREL CRAGS

OS ref. SK 582149
(Sheet 129)

SITUATION and CHARACTER

There are several small crags above the village of Mountsorrel on Castle Hill overlooking the Soar Valley. The rock is granite and the exposures are mostly small, very old, quarries. The crags currently only give bouldering in a pleasant environment. There is also an enormous quarry to the west of Mountsorrel (called Mountsorrel Quarry, Castle Hill Quarry or Main Quarry, opened 1852) which is currently being filled in. There appear to be some excellent opportunities in this quarry particularly on the SE face of the little mountain (576150) and just inside the gate on the left (above the skips). The quarry will not be completely in filled because rock exposure has to be left for the geologists. Who knows, it may be the climbable bit. The rock was capable of giving monoliths of great size and has been polished and used in buildings. Most went for kerbstones and setts for paving streets.

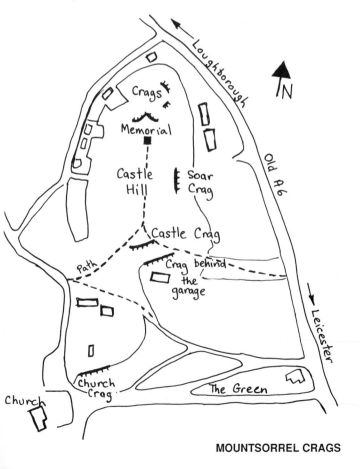

MOUNTSORREL CRAGS

APPROACH and ACCESS

Castle Hill is public open space and there are several paths giving access. There is parking beside The Green.

There appears to be no problem with access to Castle Hill and Church Crag. However, the Crag Behind the Garage is behind a garage which still operates and the area is probably private. Access to the enormous quarry that is being filled in is doubtful. However, **The Chimney** at 577151 (built 1879) looks accessible and would have 8 good 10m routes.

See map for detailed locations.

MEMORIAL CRAG

This is the best outcrop and the grass drops so steeply in places below the rock that it might be exciting to fall off. It is just below the War Memorial on the north of the hill. The small trees round it are cleared occasionally so it has an open aspect.

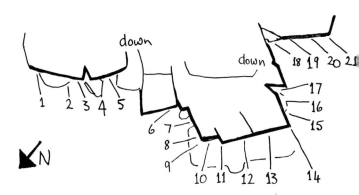

MEMORIAL CRAG

1 4c Short wall

2 4c Dome shaped slab and fierce mantleshelf.

3   Cracked wall. (Not climbed yet)

4 4c The arête with two good holds.

5 5b The wall with high left toe pocket, from the very bottom.

6 5a The thin crack, swing toe onto slab, and then up the arête.

7 5b Leaning wall, poor holds to a jug and 'monkey' finish.

8 5a Using the right arête, swing up onto leaning wall, move left and up.

9 4b Slab and arête with friction hold start.

10 3c Slab and groove.

11 4b Left edge of wall.

12 4a Up the wall.

13 4a The higher wall and continuation wall direct.
14 4b Right arête from the right.
15 4c Thin crack from right side.
16 5b The overhang direct.
17 D The corner.
18 VD Long groove.
19 4c Wall direct.
20 4c Wall direct.
21 4a The arête (there is a tree in the way at present).

SOAR CRAG

This small outcrop faces out over the Soar Valley and is just below the saddle of Castle Hill.

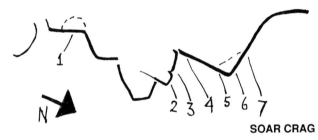

SOAR CRAG

1 4a Cracked arête from the cave.
2 D The arête.
3 3b The twin cracks.
4   The wall direct (not climbed as yet).
5   The arête (not climbed as yet).
6 4c The grooved nose.
7 VD Slab.

CASTLE CRAG

This outcrop is at the south end of the top of Castle Hill above the wall at the top of the Crag Behind the Garage. It doesn't look much but has a few problems.

1 4b Up over middle of block.
2 4a Short wall and slab direct.
3 5a Overhanging wall and slab 'Vote No'.
4 3c Corner.
5 4c Arête and wall.
6 4a Corner.
7 5b Crack and arête.
8 3a Nose and corner.

CASTLE CRAG

CRAG BEHIND THE GARAGE

This good-looking crag lies just over the wall below Castle Crag. The wall is to stop you falling over it. It obviously has several routes but, also very obviously, would be difficult to climb on without being noticed by the owner.

CHURCH CRAG

This little crag also looks good. It is opposite the church, with public open space beneath. It is overgrown but, facing south, is clean and dry. If the vegetation were cleared it would be an excellent little crag of 5m or so.

NOTES

There are several old quarries around Mountsorrel and the area would be worth investigating. However, the whole area is still active because the enormous Buddon Quarry is still in full production. There is Hawcliff Quarry (573152) with some stunning grooves and walls rising straight out of the water and Cocklow Quarry (570152) but both are within the Buddon Quarry works.

FLAT ROCK near OAKS PINNACLE

NUNCKLEY QUARRY

OS ref. SK569143
(Sheet 129)

SITUATION and CHARACTER

This was wrongly called Kinchley Hill Quarry in the old guide. Nunckley Quarry is a small disused granite quarry situated just north of the old railway line which branches off the Great Central Railway at the south end of Swithland Reservoir and which once led through the main Mountsorrel quarries over the river Soar on a fine bridge and on to Barrow on Soar.

The quarry is currently a bit overgrown but there is a splendid south-facing buttress of 20m or so. The foot of this buttress is blocked by an overhanging wall which, although only 3m high and 8m long looks very hard indeed. It is unclimbed. The upper section contains some pleasant looking grooves. The rock is very similarly to that of Craig Buddon.

APPROACH and ACCESS

The back road from Rothley Station to Quorn crosses the old railway at a bridge about 50m north of Halstead Road. Park on the verge and take a small path to the west off the north-west corner of the bridge. There are now two possibilities. Either descend the steps to the old railway and walk (fight) through the undergrowth west for about 100m before an opening in the cutting leads north into the quarry – or boldly follow a small path to the right through the undergrowth until the main buttress can be seen. Descend a mud slope to the bottom of the quarry.

Ownership of the quarry is not at all certain; it may be old railway property or belong to the modern quarry. However, locals walk their dogs, and kids play in the scrub. There are no neighbours and so climbing here should worry no-one.

THE CLIMBS

The most obvious feature is the overhanging wall blocking access to the main buttress. The first route is left of this on a subsidiary buttress, **LEFT BUTTRESS**. Routes are described from left to right.

1 **Studio**   12m   VD
On the left of the buttress climb a vertical wall on small holds to an earth covered ledge by an awkward mantleshelf. Climb a block on the right, then move right for 3m and work upwards and left over a block of doubtful stability to the top.

Further right is a gully and then a steep upper wall. Just right is **CENTRAL BUTTRESS**. *The foot of* Central Buttress *is blocked by a long steeply overhanging wall. The next route skirts this on the right.*

2 **Bogey Wall**   20m   S   4a
Start at the right-hand side of the leaning wall. Up, skirting the overhang and bearing a little left to the foot of an obvious groove and ledge to the right of a number of small trees. Climb the groove to the top.

3 **End Slab**   7m   VD
To the right of the main face is as short slab topped by an overhanging block. Climb straight up the wall turning the overhang on the right.

NOTES

This quarry looks promising for the development of intermediate grade routes on the main buttress. There will also be desperate boulder problems on the leaning wall. Spring visitors should take a saw, reap hook and trowel. Don't climb alone. If you fall off it might be a long time before they find you.

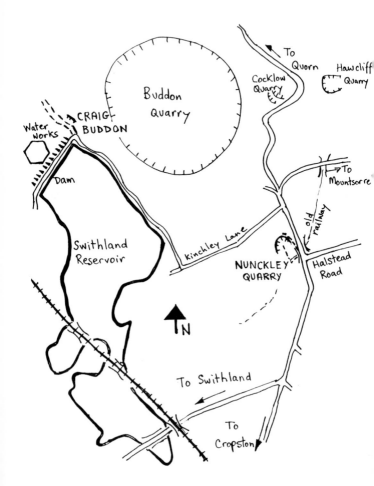

CRAIG BUDDON and NUNCKLEY QUARRY

OAKS PINNACLE

OS ref. SK467160
(Sheet 129)

SITUATION and CHARACTER

Historically called the Hanging Stone.   Unlike the Hangingstone Rocks at Woodhouse Eaves this one really is a hanging stone. A superb sight. One enormous block balanced on top of another. This is the only pinnacle of any height in Leicestershire. You can only wonder at how it came to be there as all the land surrounding it is flat (its called Flat Hill).

APPROACH and ACCESS

The Oaks Pinnacle is difficult to approach because it is so hard to park on the fast, but narrow, road that passes nearby. The nearest place is by the Lodge at the end of the drive into Charnwood Lodge. The approach is then down the drive past the "Bomb Rocks" (lumps included in an old lava flow, 463157) and across to the Pinnacle.

The Charnwood Lodge estate was left to the Leicestershire and Rutland Trust for the Nature Conservation (instead of, as was hoped, the National Trust). The Leicestershire and Rutland Trust run the estate as a nature reserve and there is no official public access.

THE CLIMBS

There are five routes on superb rough rock.

1 **Left Arête**   6m   VS   4c   *
Follow the left arête but keep your feet on the front face at all times. It is hard to get off the ground. Don't use the holds on the *Central Route*.

2 **Central Route**   6m   VS   4c   ***
A superb route going direct up the middle of the front face. Sharp holds lead you to a horizontal fist-jamming break. You can see daylight through this break. Finish by laying away up the sharp crack.

3 **Right Arête**   6m   VD   **
The classic way up and down. Climb the right arête on large, but hidden, holds. A delightful route, most difficult at the top.

4 **Left Face**   6m   VS   4c
The steep slabby left-hand face of the Pinnacle. Taken direct it is quite technical after the mid-height break.

5 **Black Back**   4m   VS   4c
The short back face provides a reach from an undercut and a slap for the jugs on the summit. This route follows *Right Arête* but on the other side.

Also two very good complete girdles — 4b with your hands in the break, 4c with the break at waist high.

To the left of the front face of the Oaks Pinnacle is a small boulder field and tor. The most prominent feature here is **FLAT ROCK**. *It is an enormous projecting, overhanging rock. Dangle from your fingertips, pull up and mantleshelf on to its flat summit (5b).*

Further towards Charnwood Lodge is a beautiful little pinnacle, **ISOLATED PINNACLE** *(467159). Although much smaller than Oaks Pinnacle it gives two good problems – the Left Face (4b) and the Right Face (4b). The real pleasure is in the quality of the rock.*

To the north of Charnwood Lodge is **COLLIER HILL** *(510610). At the south east end of a long rocky ridge amidst the trees is an overhanging wall to the right of a large ash tree. There are two strenuous cracks (4c) here. 50m west of this is an arête (4a).*

TIMBERWOOD HILL *(around 472149) has several spectacular outcrops but none have yielded much climbing.*

OAKS PINNACLE

OUTWOODS CRAG

OS ref. SK514167
(Sheet 129)

SITUATION and CHARACTER

The Outwoods Crag is a north-facing woodland outcrop of natural rock (weathered Precambrian slate agglomerate) which is slow to dry. It has several lower grade routes which make it a good crag for beginners although some of the problems are not without interest. The crag is desperately greasy on a wet winter day but catches the sun through the trees very late on a summer evening. The main characteristic of the crag is the oak tree running up the Main Face. Oak tree belays are plentiful at the top. The crag was part of a bequest by Mr Alan Moss to Loughborough Corporation in 1946 – a far-sighted action.

APPROACH and ACCESS

The quickest approach is along the track through the wood which starts on the Nanpantan/Woodhouse Eaves road near Charnwood Hall. The crag is just beside the track where the path leaves the Outwoods. The Outwoods are owned by Charnwood Borough Council and are managed by the Outwoods Management Committee. There have been no difficulties with access until lately. The area has recently been made an SSSI and the Borough Council have to monitor the use of the Outwoods by groups. Before a visit groups should phone Charnwood Borough Council (0509-263151 Ext 2102) and say they are going to climb at the Outwoods. Alternatively, visit Macaulay House, next to the Town Hall in Loughborough. The warden at the Outwoods has been known to be very outspoken to groups if he has not been informed of their visit. There are no restrictions on climbing by individuals – only monitoring of groups. The posted Bye-Laws restrict assemblies and also climbing trees (so watch it on *Monkey* or it might cost you a £5 fine).

THE CLIMBS

The main feature of the crag is the tree. The routes are described from left to right. Over on the **LEFT WING** are:

1 **Pip**   6m   D
Start at the bottom left-hand corner of the slab. Go up round the overhang on its left and finish up the slab.

2 **Roof**   6m   VD
Directly over the centre of the overhang.

3 **Squeak**   8m   D
Start in the bay. Follow the little rib in the centre of the bay to broken rocks. Finish up the arête above.

The slab at the bottom of the next rib with boulders at the foot has several problems, both on the slab and on the wall to the left.

To the right is an inverted V slab. There are several 5m problems here.

a)   3c   The overhang at the top of the slab
b)   4a   The upper of the three cracks on the right
c)   4c   The centre crack

d)   5a   The wall between the centre crack and the easy right-hand crack.

e)   5a   The wall to the right of the easy crack without using the crack or right arête

*To the right an oak tree runs up the **MAIN FACE**. There is a buttress the left of the tree.*

4 Wilfred   6m   D
Up the slab and then the left edge of the buttress.

5 Mid   6m   S
1m to the right of the edge of the buttress.

6 Split   6m   D
The obvious crack in the buttress left of the tree.

7 Twee   6m   HS
The slab between the crack and the tree. Mind your head on the tree.

8 Oak   6m   VS
An unusual route. Climb the chimney formed by the tree and the face left of the tree. Finish direct over the overhang of the tree. Some loose wood

9 Monkey   6m   VD
The tree direct! Make the Dead Man's Leap from the top.

10 Puzzle   6m   D
Climb the crack just right of the tree.

11 Clown   9m   S
The face 2m right of the tree between the two cracks.

12 Bear   9m   D
Climb the right-trending crack to the niche. Finish direct.

13 Squirrel   9m   D
Climb the thin crack direct to the niche.

14 Edge   9m   HS   4b
The right arête of the main crag direct.

15 Steps   9m   D
The staircase at the right of the main crag with the three green overhangs.

POCKETGATE QUARRY

OS ref. SK523155
(Sheet 129)

SITUATION and CHARACTER

This old slate quarry is located in a secluded wooded corner (jungle), at the north end of the Charnwood Forest Golf Course, north west of Woodhouse Eaves. The main feature is an unusual slab inclined at a deceptively shallow angle and bounded on the left by an overhanging wall – which still awaits its first routes. The crag faces north and is mostly overhung by large trees. It sees little sun, so is often green. Neglected over the last ten years, the routes are in need of use to bring them back into condition. In the meantime take a wire brush and go on a dry day. The few climbs here are all very worthwhile when dry but the slate is very slippery when wet and covered in leaves. The quarry contains ancient rare fossils. A concentric ring structure (*Charniodiscus concentricus*), the first Precambrian fossil, was discovered over a hundred years ago. More recently (1959) a frond-like structure was found. They are thought to be some form of ancient seaweed. The only other ones occur in Australia. If you find them, leave them alone. They have been there longer than you.

APPROACH and ACCESS

From Woodhouse Eaves, take the road to Nanpantan which joins the A512 half a mile on the Loughborough side of junction 23 on the M1. After passing the (lower) Beacon Hill car park on your left, with the golf course on your right, the road descends for a mile to a inconspicuous crossroads. Turn right into the lane opposite Deans Lane. The Outwoods are on your left. Park your car sensibly within the next 300m and walk keeping right along the lane bordering the golf club. The quarry is on your right hidden behind bushes and trees. The quarry is owned by the golf club. Used sensibly the climbing does not interfere with the golfers. No formal access exists, but climbers have used this quarry for over fifty years without any problems. Keep a low profile and be considerate of the situation.

HISTORY

The rock is purple in colour and was used for a facing stone. Most of the routes are nail scratched, which must date them pre-1948. Unfortunately it is not known who first climbed here. Before the golf course was purchased from the Beaumanor Estate in 1946 and access restricted (1957) this quarry and the adjacent Hangingstone Rocks, were the 'Mecca' of Leicestershire climbing.

The quarries at Woodhouse Eaves belonged to the Herrick family. They produced a stone which, although it cleaves, is not a true slate but a crystallithic tuff.

THE CLIMBS

From left to right:

1 **Lichen Buttress**   9m   D
Up the lowest part of the left-bounding wall.

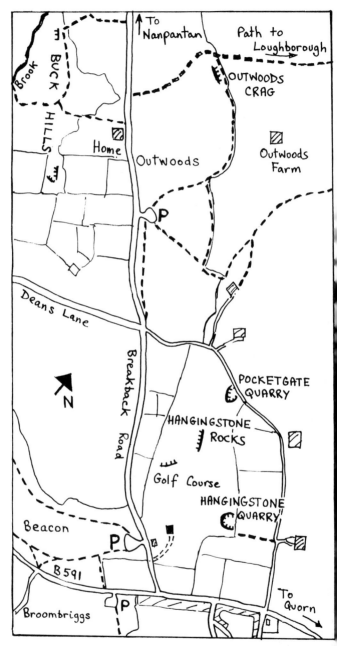

**BUCK HILLS, HANGINGSTONE QUARRY, HANGINGSTONE
ROCKS, OUTWOODS CRAG and POCKETGATE QUARRY**

2   Lamina   22m   A1

The obvious diagonal crack line across the left-bounding overhanging wall has been climbed with a number of pegs. The wall is quite extensive and offers opportunities for hard free routes.

3   Roof   25m   E1   5b

From half way up *The Wall Route* climb direct just right of a rib on sloping holds. Poor protection. *D. Jump.*

4   The Wall Route   30m   VD   ***

Start at a collection of boulders on the left of the slab. Ascend direct on small holds to the junction of the slab and the left bounding wall. Hugging the wall, move up on small flakes. Bear left at the top to finish under a large oak tree. A direct finish (S) breaks left as soon as it is possible to get onto a small slab at an upper level. Climb the slab and finish up the steep wall.

5   Slip and Slide   30m   VS   4c   **

Climb the left corner of the steep wall at the base of the slab and continue up a faint line to join *The Wall Route* at two thirds height.

6   Central Crack   30m   VS   5a   ***

Also called *All Fall Down*. The route of the crag. Start in the centre of the slab. Climb the base wall and continue until the route crosses the fault running across the slab. Move onto the upper section and proceed up the crack line. It begins to fade alarmingly and soon there is only friction and hope. Should you hear a bell ring at this point, fear not. It tolls not for thee. The golfers ring it before they drive over the blind summit. Finish up the short steep final wall to a huge tree belay. A unique climb. The only protection is off line in *The Wall Route*. E1 without it. Many have taken the long slide to the bottom and hobbled away.

7   The Pinch   27m   VS   4c   *

Also called *Fascist*. Start as for *Central Crack*. After moving onto the slab, follow a faint fault line running all the way diagonally rightwards up the slab. Finish up the head wall.

8   Ordinary Route   20m   D

The well defined crack/fault line on the right side of the slab running left to right.

9   Rightside Route   30m   HS   4a   **

Follow the junction of the slab and wall all the way, crossing the finish of *Ordinary Route* and *Central Crack*, to terminate up the top of *The Wall Route*.

10   Girdle Traverse   33m   VS   4c   *

Start in the extreme left corner of the slab. Traverse up rightwards into *The Wall Route*. Move right to gain the *Central Crack* just above the fault. Ascend for 5m then right again on almost invisible holds until the slanting crack of *Ordinary Route* is reached. Cross this on a delicate and dusty slab to a grassy ledge on *Rightside Route*. From this a swing is made up into the right bounding wall.

POCKETGATE QUARRY

SLAWSTON BRIDGE

OS ref. SP783934
(Sheet 141)

SITUATION and CHARACTER

"The Bridge" is not natural rock at all but the abutments of an old railway bridge over a road. The span has gone. Slawston Bridge has become popular as a climbing area; after all, there's not much south-east of Leicester. The bridge offers the best local climbing with numerous steep 7m fingery problems in a fine open setting. The main walls are exactly the right height – too high to treat falls in a cavalier manner, and not high enough to get seriously hurt (unless you are run over). There are three "rocks" (ironstone, gritstone and smooth blue engineers bricks). Quite why this particular bridge was built to be favourable for climbing is unclear, but others on the same railway line don't give any worthwhile climbing at all.

APPROACH and ACCESS

The bridge is about 16 miles south-east of Leicester. The quickest approach is on minor roads through Great Glen to Kibworth Harcourt, then left on minor roads through the Langtons and Welham to Weston-by-Welland. As you enter Weston, turn sharp left and follow the Slawston road for approximately 1.5 miles. The Wheel at Weston sells good beer and seems to tolerate climbers.

The bridge is on a fairly quiet public road and access is no problem. Please remember that an accident involving a vehicle might be sufficient to cause a ban on climbing.

THE CLIMBS

The layout is simple, with two vertical walls, each with right and left wings. The wings are at an easier angle. The terms **left** and **right** refer to the normal direction of approach **from the south.** The drainage pipes are a prominent feature of the **LEFT WALL**. The problems indicated on the diagrams are strangely natural, inescapable lines given by grooves, ribs and lines of weakness on the walls. Strong fingers and the ability to rest out of balance are the prerequisites. When on ribs and in grooves it is considered unethical to use holds on adjacent walls.

The grades range from 4b to 6b.

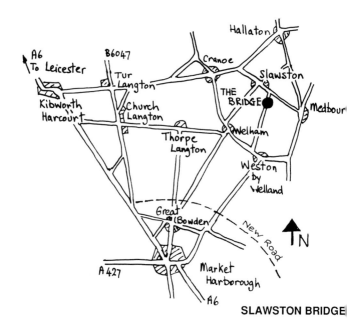

SLAWSTON BRIDGE

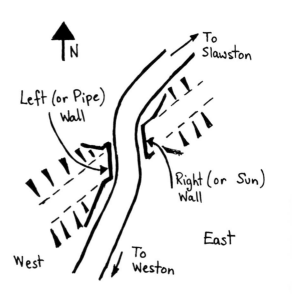

SLAWSTON BRIDGE

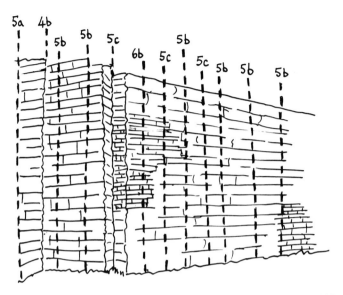

LEFT WING OF RIGHT (SUN) WALL

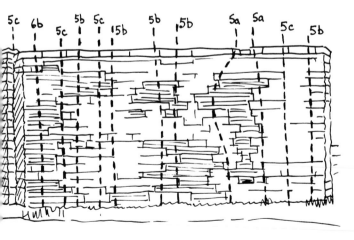

RIGHT (SUN) WALL

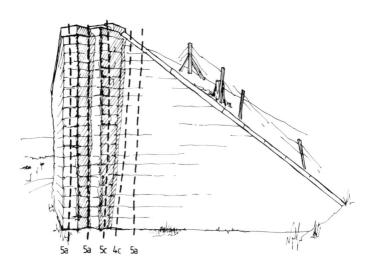

5a   5a   5c   4c   5a

RIGHT WING OF RIGHT (SUN) WALL

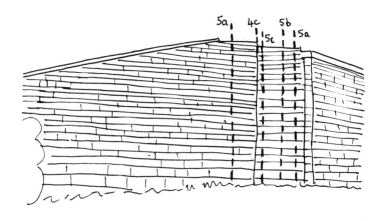

5a   4c   5b   5a
     5c

LEFT WING OF LEFT (PIPE) WALL

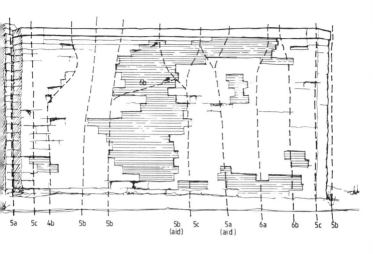

5a   5c   4b   5b   5b   5b   5c   5a   6a   6b   5c 5b
                            (aid)   (aid)

LEFT (PIPE) WALL

Tetrion Traverse (6b), SLAWSTON BRIDGE

WHITWICK QUARRY

OS ref. SK444160
(Sheet 129)

SITUATION and CHARACTER

This old granite quarry (its proper name is Forest Rock Quarry) was once the centre of climbing in Leicestershire with over 100 recorded climbs. Now, alas, most of it has been filled in and many classic routes of the early 60's and 70's have been lost. Routes such as *Pigs Ear*, *Red Wall Arête* and *Catchpenny Twist*. However, the upper half of Regalia Buttress has survived together with a large area of rock to the left. Two original high quality routes still exist. The best is *Sceptre* on Regalia Buttress which has the air of Cloggy about it.

APPROACH and ACCESS

The quarry is situated on the east side of Whitwick Village some five miles north west of Junction 22 on the M1. From junction 22 take the A50 towards Burton-on-Trent. In less than a mile turn right at a roundabout onto the B519 and follow this to Copt Oak (there is a YHA here). In Copt Oak turn left over the motorway and follow the B587 some 3 miles to Whitwick. As you pass the village sign, there is a long new stone wall on your right. After 100m turn left and park in Hastings Avenue. The low stone wall has a double action steel five-bar gate which leads onto a path. Follow this up over the landscaped area. At the top of the bank Regalia Buttress is seen to your right. Follow the rim of the quarry round to the rocks. Once you know the way it is possible to park in St. Bernards Road (the turning before Hastings Avenue) and go in through the big hole in the fence opposite. Also it is sometimes possible to park in front of the entrance gates.

The old lower quarry has been almost completely filled with overburden from the adjacent Spring Hill Quarry, owned by ARC. There is a track which links the two quarries so the area may still be covered by the Mines and Quarries Act. Tipping now appears sporadic and is well away from the old crag, and separated by a sort of moat so climbing imposes no impediment on the quarry. ARC seem to take a very laid-back attitude – they let the locals (who presumably know the blasting times) walk their dogs on the perimeter road even when the quarry is working. The crag is discrete and the local kids play on the terraces and in the trees. The crag has not been used much in recent years, because of the tipping, but now that this is nearly complete the best pitches of some excellent routes remain. There are acres of rock awaiting exploration.

THE CLIMBS

First locate Regalia Buttress with the obvious slab of *Sceptre*.

1 **The Missing Link**   15m   VS   4c
About 40m left of *Regalia Buttress* is a prominent black overhang. The bird droppings are an obvious feature. Climb up to the overhang and move up right on to the arête. This is climbed to the top. Hard for the grade owing to the loose rock. *T. Clarke and J. Cliffe, Sept. 1971.*

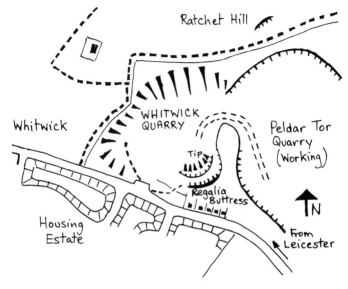

WHITWICK QUARRY

2 Link Up   29m   HVS   5a
Start 5m right of the start of *The Missing Link* at the obvious crack splitting the buttress. Climb the steep crack strenuously, pulling over the bulge to reach easier ground. Possible tree belay on right. Just left of the arête go steeply up the wall and move on to the arête at 7m (old peg runner). Pull over the small overhang and climb the loose easy groove and slab to the top. *B. Courtney and S. Taylor, 26 July 1977.*

The routes on **REGALIA BUTTRESS** *are described from left to right.*

Some 30m to the left of the top of the buttress of Sceptre *is an area of slabs. A terrace leads down from the top. Four short routes start here.*

3 Ballot Box   6m   VD
The steep cracked groove on the left of the left edge of the slab. *1983.*

4 Date Of The Next Election   6m   HVS   5a
The finger crack on the left edge of the slab. *M. Elliott, 1983.*

5 Local Election   6m   HVS   5a
Climb the centre of the obvious slab. *M. Elliott, 1983.*

6 Polling Day   6m   S
The the right of the slab is a light coloured rib with a bulging start. Climb this direct. *1983.*

REGALIA BUTTRESS, Whitwick Quarry

Further to the right is the narrow slab of Sceptre.

7 **Cloud Nine**   20m   S   4a
4m left of the start of *Sceptre* is a holly tree. Climb the awkward nose (minute "up and over") to a tree stump. Climb the crack to a ledge (possible belay) and continue up the wall by the obvious fault line to the finish of *Sceptre. D.J. Jump and S. Clarke, 12 Apl, 1975.*

8 **Sceptre**   20m   VS   4c   ***
The left side of Regalia Buttress is an obvious slabby groove. Climb a lower slab by its inner edge, then the groove to finish on the exposed left edge of the slab. It is possible to traverse in from the side and miss the bottom groove. There is also a direct finish up a borehole on the right. *K.S. Vickers and G.V.W. Boulton, April 1964.*

9 **Orb**   15m   VS   4c   **
Climb the bulging left edge of the buttress right of *Sceptre.*

10 **The Wezzock**   10m   S
Right of the bottom of *Sceptre* is a small buttress. Ascend the right-hand wall from the lowest point. Make an awkward move halfway on to the sloping shelf and continue to the top via the arête.

There are also short problems on natural granite on the face overlooking the gardens to the south.

WHITWICK ROCKS

OS ref. SK437164
(Sheet 129)

SITUATION and CHARACTER

The Rocks are situated in Whitwick village on Cademan Street. It is unfortunate that the crag is so awkwardly sited but the quality of the granite does much to counteract this. This crag was wrongly named in the 1966 guide. It was also wrongly called Peldar Tor in the 1973 edition (Peldar Tor is along the road on the way to Leicester). The Rocks are very old, being mentioned as belonging to the Parish of Swannington in 1835. It is likely, but uncerain, that the place was once called Pinfold Quarry. It has also been referred to as Whitwick Village Quarry.

The crag has become overgrown with trees and has assorted ex-lorry junk at the foot. Old photographs show the Rocks as a prominent feature of the village. It is a pity they are becoming overgrown.

APPROACH and ACCESS

The Rocks are an old quarry and Aucott's Garage is at the foot. The garage owners, two brothers, do not wish the crag to be climbed on, but it is possible that it is not theirs. The quarry was once owned by the Parish, and current ownership is not clear (the Church?). Certainly in the past kids used to scramble up it on the way to school. Visits have been made early (6-7 am) on sunny summer Sunday mornings.

WHITWICK ROCKS

THE CLIMBS

1 Green Slab 8m S 4a
The crag furthest from the road, rising from the undergrowth at the back of the garages. Ascend a green slab to the right of a small overhang to a square projecting block. From the top of the block go diagonally right across the slab to the top by an obvious route.

2 Flypaper 5m S 4a
A corner with a slab on the left and an overhang on the right. Climb the slab direct.

3 Left Arête 8m S 4c
The left rib of the large obvious square cut overhanging corner, a peg for aid.

4 Quaver 9m VS 4c   *
The large overhanging corner in two sections. Ascend the first section direct with interest, then move left up the smooth vertical wall, and easier ground to the top. Or after the first section move up right over the leaning wall on good jugs. A pleasant enough climb. *K.S. Vickers, S. Gregory and D.N. Draper, Oct. 1963.*

5 Right Arête 6m VD
Up the right arête to the top.

6 Rag Slab 9m D
The broken slab 8m left of a stone wall at right angles to the road.

7 Brewery Wall 9m HS 4b
The black overhanging corner immediately above the stone wall.

8 Bus Stop 9m VD
The obvious arête near the road, difficult in the upper half.

9 Final Wall 9m VD
The wall immediately on the right. Climb delicately up the centre of the wall finishing by an awkward mantleshelf.

*The **CRAG OPPOSITE** is on the other side of the road and has an excellent steep clean wall about 7m high beside a small warehouse. Ownership is unknown.*

INDEX

THE POWER OF THE STONE

This guide was finished when we found that there was a blank page. The following piece by Roger Ramsbottom just fits:

The most mysterious place in Charnwood Forest is the Hanging Stone near Oaks in Charnwood. Hardly anyone has heard of it and very few have visited it. It is a secret place. Very few have been there on nights when the full moon illuminates the eerie flat landscape. On the one night a year when the instant of the full moon occurs during the darkness of a Sunday the Power of The Stone is said to be at its greatest.

In T.R. Potters book "The History and Antiquities of Charnwood Forest" (1842) there is a mention of the spot. "No one riding up to the lower side of The Stone on a spirited horse can fail to notice the emotion of the animal; Mr. Gisbourne's Scotch Cattle, on their first arrival, always gaze at it with wonder. An old forester told me "I always take care never to be near it after twilight has begun". Potter also attached significance to the fact that a quern, or hand-mill, was found on Kite Hill in the vicinity. He also noted that the centre of the triangle formed by Tynte (Tin) Meadows, Kite Hill, and The Stone was locally known as "The Grove", a name suggestive of ancient rites of worship.

The rock of The Stone is some of the most ancient in Britain, and is very near the centre of England. A remarkable number of buildings, particularly churches, has been built on alignments of The Stone with prominent Charnwood hills.

i)   the Temple of Venus in Garendon Park was built on an exact line from The Stone through Ives Head and with a distance ratio of one to two

ii) the ruins of the chapel on Temple Hill were built to exactly align with The Stone and Mount Saint Bernards Abbey

iii) the Calvary in the Abbey aligns through The Stone with Beacon Hill

iv) the chapel at Grace Dieu Manor aligns through The Stone with Gun Hill

v)   The old chapel near Old Hall Farm was built to align through Bardon Hill with The Stone

vi) The Catholic Church at Whitwick aligns with Charley Knoll and The Stone

vii) the Church at Oaks in Charnwood exactly aligns through The Stone with the church in Coalville. The ancient site at Tin (or Tynte) Meadow completes this remarkable alignment of four.

The University of Leicester have investigated the emanations from the ground around The Stone.

The Oaks is probably the oldest settlement in the Forest. The power of The Stone kept Christianity at bay until the Oaks in Charnwood Church (the first of the Charnwood churches, the others being at Markfield and Woodhouse Eaves) was built less than a mile away (in the middle of nowhere) in 1815. But even this couldn't still the power of the place and in the 1840's the Catholic Abbey, with its complement of full-time monks, was sited on a nearby knoll to oversee The Stone.

There is a local tradition that lads must climb The Stone before any girl will take them in wedlock.

Climb at twilight. Feel the Power.

More local outdoor recreation books from CORDEE

WALKS AROUND CHARNWOOD   Heather MacDermid   £3.95

A guide for walkers wishing to explore the ancient tracks and footpaths of
Charnwood Forest. Within a 30 mile circuit, five inner circular routes of
six, eight or ten miles are described. Clear and concise instructions for
walking the route are accompanied by a simplified strip map which travels
each page.
96 pages, 125 c 175mm

FOXTON LOCKS TO RUTLAND WATER
— FAVOURITE WALKS   Heather MacDermid   £4.95

This book takes you on the authors favourite walks through the beautiful
but less well known countryside of east Leicestershire. You can choose
the length of walk that suits you best. Choose a short walk of 4 or 5 miles
stopping to explore as you go along: or add on another circuit to make a
long figure of eight if you like.
148 pages, 125 x 175mm

EAST MIDLANDS RIVER GUIDE   Colin Broadway   £4.95

A canoeists' guide to the rivers and canals of the East Midlands. The area
is best known for the Nottingham Watersports Centre, but also contains
pheasant rural touring rivers in summer, and exciting paddling in winter
floods.
88 pages, 210 x 148mm

These books are available from the shops or can be ordered directly from
Cordee, 3a De Montfort Street, Leicester LE1 7HD (please add 10%
postage).

Please write for a copy of our comprehensive stocklist of climbing and
outdoor recreation/travel books and maps, some 3000 different titles.

Steve Etherington on Plain Sailing (E2), **MARKFIELD QUARRY**
Photo: Tony Charles

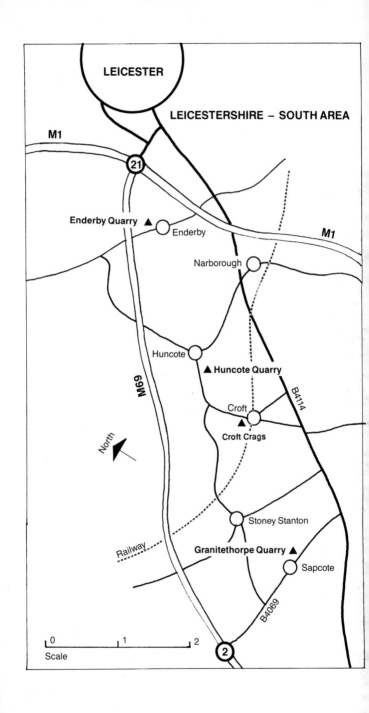